Learning Devise for Rails

Use Devise to make your Rails application accessible, user friendly, and secure

Hafiz

Nia Mutiara

Giovanni Sakti

[PACKT] open source
PUBLISHING
community experience distilled

BIRMINGHAM - MUMBAI

Learning Devise for Rails

First published: October 2013

Production Reference: 1181013

Published by Packt Publishing Ltd.
Livery Place
35 Livery Street
Birmingham B3 2PB, UK.

ISBN 978-1-78216-704-4

www.packtpub.com

Cover Image by Suresh Mogre (suresh.mogre.99@gmail.com)

Credits

Authors
Hafiz
Nia Mutiara
Giovanni Sakti

Reviewers
Philip Hallstrom
Andrew Montgomery-Hurrell
Akshay Surve

Acquisition Editors
Nikhil Karkal
Taron Pereira

Commissioning Editor
Neil Alexander

Technical Editors
Jalasha D'costa
Tarunveer Shetty

Copy Editors
Mradula Hegde
Dipti Kapadia
Sayanee Mukherjee

Project Coordinator
Amigya Khurana

Proofreader
Linda Morris

Indexer
Mehreen Deshmukh

Production Coordinator
Aparna Bhagat

Cover Work
Aparna Bhagat

About the Authors

Hafiz majored in Informatics Engineering at Bandung Institute of Technology, Bandung. He graduated in 2008. In his study period, he spent most of his time researching user interaction. It was a bit contradictive because he worked mainly in backend programming after he graduated. Most of his research was about ActionScript, PHP, and Javascript. About 2 years later, he came across Ruby on Rails, which sparked a lot more interest in web development. His interest was magnified after he took on the role of Chief Technology Officer in a startup (Wiradipa Nusantara) he built with his friends. Since then, most of his time was contributed to research on Ruby, Ruby on Rails, and web performance. He blogs extensively about Ruby and Ruby on Rails at `http://hafizbadrie.wordpress.com`. He has written a lot about best practices for using Ruby on Rails and also about web performance.

Currently, he is a Lead Developer in The Jakarta Post Digital while maintaining his startup as a CTO in Wiradipa Nusantara. In recent days, he is paying more attention to the development of web performance from the server side with Ruby, the client side with JavaScript, and any other related strategy. He is a member of id-ruby (`http://id-ruby.org`), an Indonesian community that talks about Ruby and is also a member of Card to Post (`http://www.cardtopost.com`), an Indonesian community that mainly talks about postcards.

My sincere gratitude to Allah. An article on Standard Widget Toolkit (SWT) brought Ashish Bhanushali to my blog and that's where the offer for this book came from. I'd like to thank the Packt Publishing team for their patience and hard work and Giovanni and Nia for making a good team—we should do this again sometime. I also want to thank my father, mother, brothers, Adelia, and all of the team in Wiradipa Nusantara for your support. I dedicate this book to all developers—not just Ruby on Rails developers—and hope it is useful to everyone who reads it.

Nia Mutiara is a software engineer working on a virtual stock gaming iOS application, as well as its server-side web application. For two years, she worked on complex Ruby on Rails and iOS applications. She is a master of JavaScript and CSS, and has used those skills to enhance most web applications that she has worked on. In her spare time, she hangs around Twitter, writes Ruby tutorials in Indonesian, and watches comedy.

Giovanni Sakti has been a developer for 10 years with an emphasis on developing web applications in Java and Ruby. His latest projects and research are focused on API-based web applications with AngularJS as the client-side framework.

He is an active member of the Indonesian Ruby (id-ruby) community and sometimes gives talks about Ruby-related topics there. He writes regularly on his blog —`http://mightygio.com`— primarily about Ruby, Rails, AngularJS, and other programming topics.

Giovanni is the founder of PT. Starqle Indonesia, a Jakarta-based company providing products, IT consulting, and development services with a focus on the healthcare industry.

I would like to thank Hafiz and Nia for giving me the opportunity to write this book together. I would also like to dedicate this book to my wife, Elvira, and to my grandmother, father, mother, and sisters, Emmy, Tri, Tina, and Livia. Lastly, I want to send my regards to everyone who shares the same dreams at PT. Starqle Indonesia.

About the Reviewers

Philip Hallstrom has been building web applications for the last 19 years. He enjoys working in the world of open source, particularly with Linux, Ruby, Rails, and PostgreSQL. He lives in Olympia, WA with his wife and two boys. When he's not on the golf course, Philip is the CTO for Supreme Golf, a startup looking to make it easy for golfers to find the best tee times available. You can find him online at `http://pjkh.com`.

Andrew Montgomery-Hurrell is a software developer, hacker, and all-round geek who enjoys everything from Dungeons and Dragons to DevOps. At an early age, he was fascinated with computers, and after cutting his teeth on BASIC with older models of Amstrad CPCs and Amigas, he moved on to Linux admin, C/C++, and then later to Python and Ruby. Since the early 2000s, he has worked on a number of web applications in a range of languages and technologies from small company catalog sites to large web applications serving thousands of people across the globe. Trained and interested in computing "from the bottom up", Andrew has experience in the full stack of computing technology—from ASICs to applications—coming from a background in electronics and computer interfacing.

When he isn't working on web applications or infrastructure tools for gaming events by hosting company, Multiplay, he can be found hacking code, reading or writing fiction, playing computer games, or slaying dragons with his wife, Laura.

Akshay Surve is in pursuit of making a difference through his initiatives, be it for profit or for good. He has a deep understanding of the Consumer Internet, Advertising, and Technology domains having worked with high-growth startups globally. At heart, he is a midnight code junkie and occasionally dabbles in prose. When not with his MacBook, he can either be found preparing for the next marathon or disappearing into the wilderness. He was once seen taking a leap from a mountain top and soaring through the skies solo in what looked like an elongated umbrella from afar.

He is the co-founder of DeltaX (`http://www.deltax.com`), where he is building "The Advertising Cloud" for advertising agencies and advertisers to efficiently buy, track, attribute, optimize, and report media across the marketing segments—search, social, display, RTB, mobile, and video.

You can connect with him on Twitter (`https://twitter.com/akshaysurve`), LinkedIn (`http://www.linkedin.com/in/akshaysurve`), his personal blog (`http://www.akshaysurve.com`), or Quora (`http://www.quora.com/Akshay-Surve`).

Akshay also self-published a book in 2012 entitled *Words are all I have* (`http://goo.gl/x2aCmV`), which is a collection of his short poems.

www.PacktPub.com

Support files, eBooks, discount offers and more

You might want to visit www.PacktPub.com for support files and downloads related to your book.

Did you know that Packt offers eBook versions of every book published, with PDF and ePub files available? You can upgrade to the eBook version at www.PacktPub.com and as a print book customer, you are entitled to a discount on the eBook copy. Get in touch with us at service@packtpub.com for more details.

At www.PacktPub.com, you can also read a collection of free technical articles, sign up for a range of free newsletters and receive exclusive discounts and offers on Packt books and eBooks.

PACKTLIB™

http://PacktLib.PacktPub.com

Do you need instant solutions to your IT questions? PacktLib is Packt's online digital book library. Here, you can access, read and search across Packt's entire library of books.

Why Subscribe?

- Fully searchable across every book published by Packt
- Copy and paste, print and bookmark content
- On demand and accessible via web browser

Free Access for Packt account holders

If you have an account with Packt at www.PacktPub.com, you can use this to access PacktLib today and view nine entirely free books. Simply use your login credentials for immediate access.

Table of Contents

Preface

Imagine that you create a cool Rails web application that does different things for different users. To do so, your application needs to be able to identify users (at least users who are logged in versus anonymous visitors) to restrict its many functionalities. Before building your core Rails application logic, you will need a few authentication-related features working, that is, sign-up, sign-in, sign-out, remember me, and password reset features. In future, you will want to integrate the login with social networking sites such as Facebook or Twitter, so that your users will not need to retype all their details when signing up for, or signing in, to your web application.

You get so excited with your Rails web application idea that you start searching online for authentication solutions. Spending your time around the Internet, you find two choices; you can roll your own authentication or pick a gem that does authentication. After weighing these choices, you realize that you need a solution that works straight away. There are multiple gems that you can pick, such as Devise, Sorcery, and AuthLogic. Considering that you want to add a social networking sign in and manage user restrictions, you want the solution to work well with the features you will add in the future.

You can get Devise (`https://github.com/plataformatec/devise`), one of the most popular authentication solutions for Rails. It is a one-stop authentication solution that works right away. It also works neatly with other gems to help you with social networking sign in and restricting resources for different users.

In this book, you will find your all-in-one guide to learn implementation of user authentication using Devise. Through a series of hands-on instructions and code examples, this book will explain how Devise saves you from having to implement different types of authentication (for example, logging in, logging out, and password resets). You will learn how flexible, customizable, and testable Devise is. This book will also show you how using Devise, together with other gems, can help you define user privileges to restrict resources and integrate a social network login with your application.

What this book covers

Chapter 1, Devise – Authentication Solution for Ruby on Rails, introduces Devise as one of the most modular, customizable authentication solutions for your Rails project. It will cover Devise setup to allow quick user login for your Rails project via e-mail.

Chapter 2, Authenticating Your Application with Devise, digs Devise customizability further down. This chapter explains the overriding of Devise controllers to tailor different needs. You will also discover how to leverage default Devise authentication view templates such as views for sign-in, edit account, and sign-up.

Chapter 3, Privileges, explains four simple steps to take advantage of the CanCan gem for defining authorization rules on what users can and cannot do on different controllers and views. It will then cover other ways to use CanCan for complex authorization rules.

Chapter 4, Remote Authentication with Devise and OmniAuth, teaches you how to enable remote authentication in your application using OmniAuth. Remote authentication provides users with the ability to sign in using third-party accounts such as Twitter and Facebook, instead of the typical username and password combination. This feature is important when you want to simplify the authentication process in your application.

Chapter 5, Testing Devise, shows you ways of testing your Devise-related code to ensure that your Rails web application is working as expected. Tests are useful for maintaining your application, especially when you expect to add lots of functionalities.

What you need for this book

As this book will guide you through plenty of hands-on examples, you should make sure that you prepare your computer for trying out the examples. One of the following operating systems is recommended:

- Ubuntu, Linux, or any UNIX-compatible OS (any version)
- Mac OS X (10.6 or higher)
- Microsoft Windows (XP or higher)

In addition, one of the following database engines should be installed on your computer:

- MySQL (latest version)
- SQLite (latest version)
- MongoDB (latest version)

Lastly, you should have the following version of Ruby on Rails installed:

- Ruby (2.0.0 or higher)
- Rails (4.0 or higher)

Who this book is for

This book is for web developers who are getting started with Rails and are looking for authentication solutions, as well as for Rails developers who are looking to extend their implementation of authentication with capabilities such as authorization and remote authentication. A fundamental understanding of Rails is required; readers should already be familiar with a few important Rails components such as bundler, migrations, models, views, and controllers. Basic knowledge of relational databases such as Ruby, HTML, and CSS is also required.

Conventions

In this book, you will find a number of styles of text that distinguish between different kinds of information. Here are some examples of these styles, and an explanation of their meaning.

Code words in text are shown as follows:

"The first thing that should be done is to add a devise gem to your `Gemfile` file."

A block of code is set as follows:

```
class User < ActiveRecord::Base
# Include default devise modules. Others available
# are:
# :token_authenticatable, :encryptable,
# :confirmable, :lockable, :timeoutable and
# :omniauthable
devise :database_authenticatable, :registerable,
:recoverable, :rememberable, :trackable,
:validatable

end
```

When we wish to draw your attention to a particular part of a code block, the relevant lines or items are set in bold:

```
class HomeController < ApplicationController
before_filter :authenticate_user!

def index
end
end
```

Any command-line input or output is written as follows:

```
$ rails generate controller home index
```

New terms and **important words** are shown in bold. Words that you see on the screen, in menus or dialog boxes for example, appear in the text like this: "Very often, when you visit the login page of a website, you will see the text **Remember Me** with a checkbox beside it."

> Warnings or important notes appear in a box like this.

> Tips and tricks appear like this.

Reader feedback

Feedback from our readers is always welcome. Let us know what you think about this book—what you liked or may have disliked. Reader feedback is important for us to develop titles that you really get the most out of.

To send us general feedback, simply send an e-mail to `feedback@packtpub.com`, and mention the book title via the subject of your message.

If there is a topic that you have expertise in and you are interested in either writing or contributing to a book, see our author guide on `www.packtpub.com/authors`.

Customer support

Now that you are the proud owner of a Packt book, we have a number of things to help you to get the most from your purchase.

Downloading the example code

You can download the example code files for all Packt books you have purchased from your account at `http://www.packtpub.com`. If you purchased this book elsewhere, you can visit `http://www.packtpub.com/support` and register to have the files e-mailed directly to you.

Errata

Although we have taken every care to ensure the accuracy of our content, mistakes do happen. If you find a mistake in one of our books—maybe a mistake in the text or the code—we would be grateful if you would report this to us. By doing so, you can save other readers from frustration and help us improve subsequent versions of this book. If you find any errata, please report them by visiting `http://www.packtpub.com/submit-errata`, selecting your book, clicking on the **errata submission form** link, and entering the details of your errata. Once your errata are verified, your submission will be accepted and the errata will be uploaded on our website, or added to any list of existing errata, under the Errata section of that title. Any existing errata can be viewed by selecting your title from `http://www.packtpub.com/support`.

Piracy

Piracy of copyright material on the Internet is an ongoing problem across all media. At Packt, we take the protection of our copyright and licenses very seriously. If you come across any illegal copies of our works, in any form, on the Internet, please provide us with the location address or website name immediately so that we can pursue a remedy.

Please contact us at `copyright@packtpub.com` with a link to the suspected pirated material.

We appreciate your help in protecting our authors, and our ability to bring you valuable content.

Questions

You can contact us at `questions@packtpub.com` if you are having a problem with any aspect of the book, and we will do our best to address it.

1

Devise – Authentication Solution for Ruby on Rails

It was around 2 months ago that I started to dig deep into **Ruby on Rails**, when I needed a plugin to handle authentication. That time, Ruby on Rails 3 was newly published, when so many gems still hadn't updated their compatibility to Rails update, including **Authlogic**. Authlogic was the first authentication gem that I used as an authentication plugin, but I couldn't use it anymore since I had to use Rails 3 in my project. That moment brought me to **Devise**. Devise was already compatible to Rails 3 and so my research began. The research concluded:

- Devise was very easy to use. The modules were developed in a very good structure.
- Devise provided 11 modules that I could use to authenticate my application.
- Devise allowed me to customize some of its modules to meet my application requirement.

These are the reasons that strongly influenced me to develop an application with Devise. It saved my time from developing new authentication modules from scratch. Now, we have reached Ruby on Rails 4; Devise was quickly updated so that developers could use it within the new Rails environment.

Devise modules

What makes Devise truly interesting is its modularity. The following modules are provided by Devise:

- **Database Authenticatable**: This module will encrypt and store a password in the database to validate the authenticity of a user while signing in. The authentication can be done both through **POST** requests or **HTTP Basic Authentication**. This is the basic module to perform authentication with Devise.

- **Token Authenticatable**: This module enables users to sign in based on an authentication token. The token can be given through query strings or HTTP Basic Authentication.
- **Omniauthable**: Attach **OmniAuth** support to Devise. By turning this module on, your application will allow the user to sign in with external accounts such as Facebook and Twitter. We will talk about this in more detail in *Chapter 3, Privileges*.
- **Confirmable**: Attach this module to enable the confirmation mechanism. So, Devise will send an e-mail with a confirmation instruction and verify whether an account is already confirmed during the sign-in process.
- **Recoverable**: There are times when users forget their passwords and need to recover it. This module is the answer for that need. Devise will allow the user to reset passwords and it will send the user the instructions via e-mail.
- **Registerable**: You can control whether or not your application provides the registration mechanism by using this module. This module is also used to allow users to edit and destroy their accounts.
- **Rememberable**: It's very often, when you visit a login page of a website, you will see a sentence, **Remember Me**, with a checkbox beside it. It will be used to remember the logged-in user by storing a cookie. In Devise, you can implement this method by attaching this module.
- **Trackable**: For certain websites, the sign-in tracker is very useful. The data can be very helpful to retrieve some information. If you choose Devise to handle your authorization mechanisms, you will be able to do it. Devise provides this module to track sign-in processes, so a user can collect information regarding sign-in count, timestamps, and the IP address.
- **Timeoutable**: This module is used to limit the session, so it will expire in a specified period of time if it has no activity.
- **Validatable**: This module provides the basic validation for e-mail and password. The validations can be customized, so you're able to define your own validations.
- **Lockable**: If you are willing to add more security to your application, this module could be very handy. Lockable will manage the maximum count of failed sign-in attempts. When it reaches the maximum number, Devise will lock the account. The user can unlock it via e-mail or after a specified time period.

These 11 modules are the essence of Devise. With these modules, you can do anything related to application authorization, which is very useful in modern applications.

Installation

We are going to learn how to install this interesting authorization plugin to your Rails application. For your information, this is the specification of application sample that I used:

- Rails 4 (4.0.0)
- Devise 3 (3.0.3)
- SQLite 3 (1.3.8)

Let's create our Rails application by executing this command:

```
$ rails new learning-devise
```

The first thing that should be done is you need to add the Devise gem to your `Gemfile`.

```
gem 'devise'
```

To make sure that everything is installed properly, you can execute the following command inside your Rails application folder:

```
$ bundle install
```

The command will install the Devise gem, and now you have to install the configuration files for Devise. You can install it all at once by executing the following command:

```
$ rails generate devise:install
```

The result of the command is shown in the following screenshot:

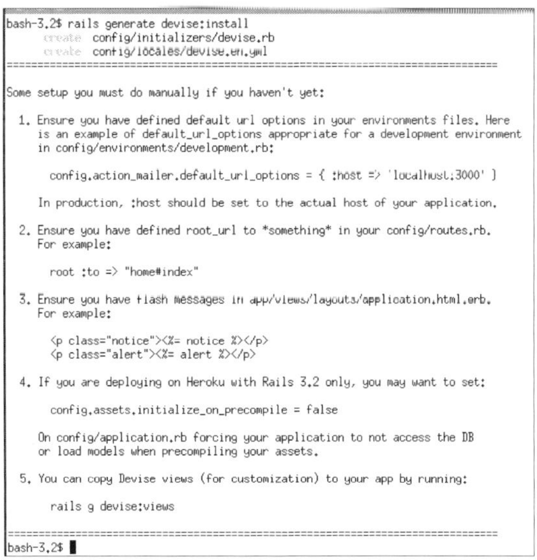

Devise installation

As you can see from the screenshot, Devise generates two new files in your Rails application. Those two files are:

- `devise.rb`: This file is located at `config/initializers/devise.rb` and will be used as the Devise main configuration file.
- `devise.en.yml`: This file is located at `config/locales/devise.en.yml` and it will be used as an internationalization file for English language.

Not just generating files, the installation command also prints some information that will be useful for our complete Devise setup. This information will tell us about:

- The basic URL configuration that applies to every environment setting. The code shown in the screenshot should be added to the environment settings, so that Devise will acknowledge the application URL which is used in its autogenerated e-mail. Especially for production, the host value should be filled with your actual application domain.
- The route setting that you need to add to your `config/routes.rb` file. By defining your root URL, Devise will use it for its redirection. For example, Devise will redirect the user to the root URL after they sign out from the application.
- Devise helpers that can be used to generate errors or warning messages when there's something wrong with the code. This is very useful and you can write it in your views file.
- Configuration that you need to add when deploying to Heroku. I'm not going to discuss about it in this book.
- How to generate copies of Devise views, so that you can customize it later. We will see how it works in *Chapter 2, Authenticating Your Application with Devise*.

The next step is generating a Devise model. Let's name our Devise model as **user**. For your information, this model name can be replaced with any name you wish. This name also determines the Devise helper's name. We will see how we use it later in this chapter. To generate the Devise model, you can execute the following command:

```
$ rails generate devise user
```

The result of this command can be seen in the following screenshot:

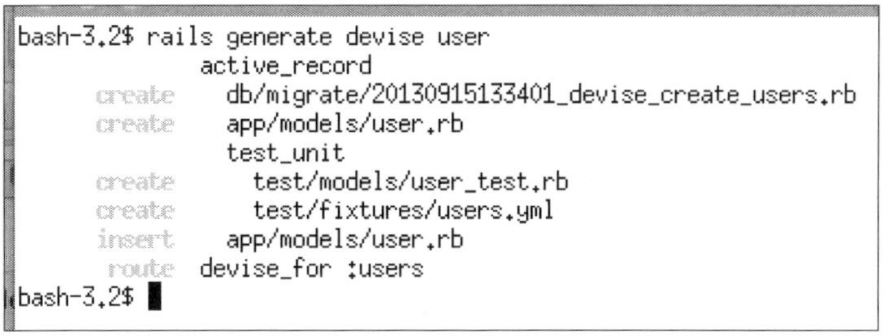

Generate Devise model

Based on the previous screenshot, Devise generates four kinds of files:

- The first kind is used as a migration file. This file is shown as `db/migrate/20130915133401_devise_create_users.rb`. Like the other migration files, it is used to generate tables in our database.
- A model file that is shown as `app/models/user.rb`.
- A test file that is shown as `test/models/user_test.rb`. This file is used to perform testing. We will discuss this topic in *Chapter 5, Testing Devise*.
- A fixture file that is shown as `test/fixtures/users.yml`. This file is used to perform testing. We will discuss this topic in *Chapter 5, Testing Devise*.

The command also modifies the model file to attach the default modules and the route file (`routes.rb`). Devise modifies the route so the application recognizes some routes generated by Devise. This is the code which is added by Devise to the route file:

```
devise_for :users
```

Now, let's open a user model file (`user.rb`) and you're going to see this code:

```
class User < ActiveRecord::Base
# Include default devise modules. Others available
# are:
# :token_authenticatable, :encryptable,
# :confirmable, :lockable, :timeoutable and
# :omniauthable
devise :database_authenticatable, :registerable,
:recoverable, :rememberable, :trackable,
:validatable

end
```

From the code, we will know that Devise will attach some default modules such as Database Authenticable, Registerable, Recoverable, Rememberable, Trackable, and Validatable. As I wrote earlier in this chapter, I suppose you already knew what the modules are for.

At this point, you have prepared all the basic settings that a Rails application needs to implement Devise. So, the next step is creating the table on your database by migrating the migration file. If you don't make any change to the Devise migration file, it means Devise will only generate columns for its default modules. But, if you make some changes like commenting on other modules such as `t.encryptable`, `t.confirmable`, `t.lockable`, and `t.tocken_authenticatble`, you will have extra columns in your user's table that will handle some specific Devise modules. So, it depends on your requirement whether you are going to use the modules or not.

We have prepared our migration file, now let's create the table. I presume that you already have the database and have prepared the database configuration at `config/database.yml`. If so, all you need to do is execute this command:

```
$ rake db:migrate
```

Now, you have prepared everything to make Devise run smoothly on your Rails application. But, there's one more thing that I want to show you. It's about how to wrap controllers with your authorization and see it in action.

Run your first application with Devise

In this section, we are going to talk about how to wrap your controllers with Devise authorization and use some Devise helper in your views. First, I want to generate a single controller by executing this command:

```
$ rails generate controller home index
```

This command will generate the controller (`home_controller.rb`) with an action named `index`. It also generates a view file located at `views/home/index.html.erb`. Let's start by opening the controller file and add a code (`:authenticate_user!`) between class definition and first action definition. Why `:authenticate_user!`? As I stated before, we have our Devise model named as user and this code is one of the Devise helpers that I meant. So, in the future, when you have a Devise model with a different name, you can change the user part in the code with your actual model name. According to our example, the controller code will be like the following:

```
class HomeController < ApplicationController
before_filter :authenticate_user!
```

```
  def index
  end
end
```

By adding the highlighted code, your Rails application will run the controller filter, which is executed before executing all the actions defined in the controller. You can also modify the filter so that it will be executed only for all actions using `:only` or `:except` code. By adding this code, you will be able to define which actions should be authorized and which should not. For example, it will be like the following code:

```
class HomeController < ApplicationController
  before_filter :authenticate_user!, :only => [:index, :new]

  def index
  end

  def new
  end

  def edit
  end
end
```

The code shows that the actions `index` and `new` are authorized, so users need to sign in before getting into the action page.

Now, let's start our Rails server by executing the command `$ rails server`. See it in action by visiting `http://localhost:3000`. The application will automatically redirect you to the sign-in page, like this:

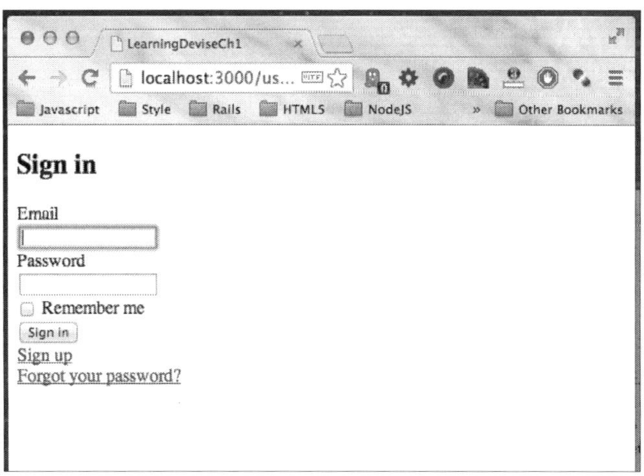

First Devise application

Now, you have run your first application with Devise. With current modules, you can only perform sign-in, sign-up, reset password, remember me action, and sign-in tracker. We will play with other modules in the next chapters, but before that, I want to show some Devise's helpers, which are very helpful in view files. Those helpers are as follows:

- `current_user`: This helper will be very useful to get the data model of a currently logged-in user. With this method, you are able to retrieve data stored in the database anytime you want it. For example, if I want to get the e-mail of the current logged-in user, I can retrieve it by calling the method `current_user.email`.
- `user_signed_in?`: This helper returns a Boolean data type, which determines whether a user is logged-in or not. For example, with this method you can hide and show sign-out link in your view. Here is the sample code for this case (`app/views/home/index.html.erb`):

```
<h1>Home#index</h1>
<p>Find me in app/views/home/index.html.erb</p>
<br>

<% if user_signed_in? %>
  <%= link_to 'Sign Out', destroy_user_session_path, method:
:delete %>
<% end %>
```

- `user_session`: This is a session variable that can set anything you want in a hash format. Actually, this helper contains the subset of the Ruby on Rails session data. So, the purpose of this helper is to simplify the use of Rails sessions. Despite using the `session` variable for every Devise model that you have, you can utilize the session helper, so the session grouping for your model will be clear. For example, I want to save a string inside the session helper, I can do it by writing this code:

```
user_session[:hello] = "world"
```

These helpers are the ones that I mentioned before. The actual name is based on your Devise model name. So, when you create or use another model name, you can use all these helpers by replacing the **user** keyword in the helpers name with the one that you have.

Summary

At this point, you've known how to set up Devise at your Rails application, saw it in action, and the helpers from Devise. We're going to dig deeper into Devise and I'm sure, if you've understood all of this, the following chapters will be easier for you.

2

Authenticating Your Application with Devise

A "state of the art" application sometimes requires more customizations from Devise, such as customization for signing in, updating accounts, resetting a user's password, or account confirmation. When you first install Devise with its default settings, you will not get these features. That's why you will need to dig deeper to have a more comprehensive understanding about Devise.

Signing in using authentication other than e-mails

By default, Devise only allows e-mails to be used for authentication. For some people, this condition will lead to the question, "What if I want to use some other field besides e-mail? Does Devise allow that?" The answer is yes; Devise allows other attributes to be used to perform the sign-in process.

For example, I will use `username` as a replacement for e-mail, and you can change it later with whatever you like, including `userlogin`, `adminlogin`, and so on. We are going to start by modifying our user model. Create a migration file by executing the following command inside your project folder:

```
$ rails generate migration add_username_to_users username:string
```

This command will produce a file, which is depicted by the following screenshot:

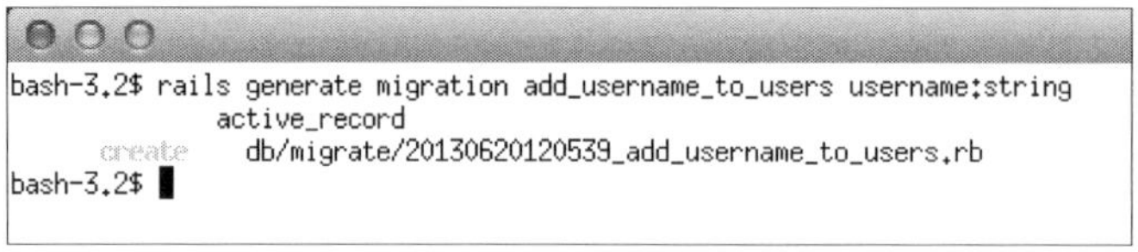

The generated migration file

Execute the migrate (`rake db:migrate`) command to alter your `users` table, and it will add a new column named `username`. You need to open the Devise's main configuration file at `config/initializers/devise.rb` and modify the code:

```
config.authentication_keys = [:username]
config.case_insensitive_keys = [:username]
config.strip_whitespace_keys = [:username]
```

You have done enough modification to your Devise configuration, and now you have to modify the Devise views to add a `username` field to your sign-in and sign-up pages. By default, Devise loads its views from its gemset code. The only way to modify the Devise views is to generate copies of its views. This action will automatically override its default views. To do this, you can execute the following command:

```
$ rails generate devise:views
```

It will generate some files, which are shown in the following screenshot:

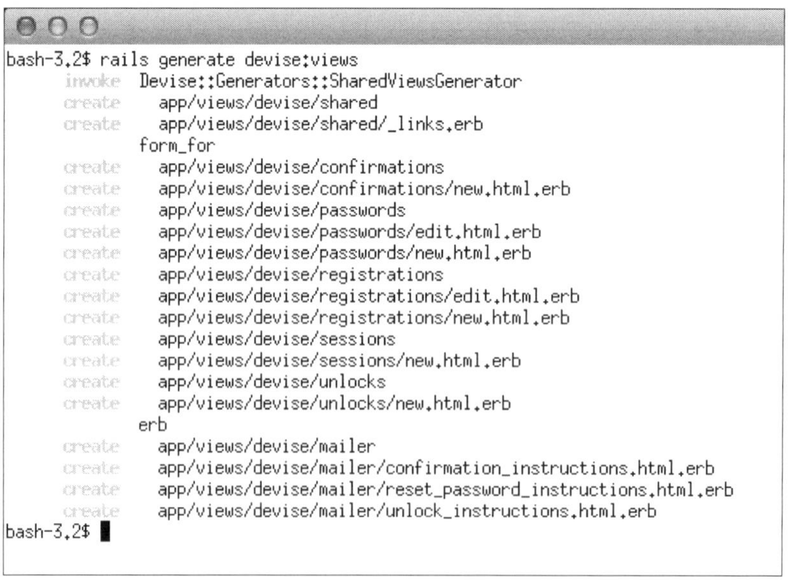

Devise views files

As I have previously mentioned, these files can be used to customize another view. But we are going to talk about it a little later in this chapter. Now, you have the views and you can modify some files to insert the `username` field. These files are listed as follows:

- `app/views/devise/sessions/new.html.erb`: This is a view file for the sign-up page. Basically, all you need to do is change the `email` field into the `username` field.

```
#app/views/devise/sessions/new.html.erb

<h2>Sign in</h2>

<%= notice %>
<%= alert %>

<%= form_for(resource, :as => resource_name, :url => session_
path(resource_name)) do |f| %>
<div><%= f.label :username %><br />
<%= f.text_field :username, :autofocus => true %><div>

<div><%= f.label :password %><br />
<%= f.password_field :password %></div>

<% if devise_mapping.rememberable? -%>
<div><%= f.check_box :remember_me %> <%= f.label :remember_me %></
div>
<% end -%>

<div><%= f.submit "Sign in" %></div>
<% end %>

%= render "devise/shared/links" %>
```

You are now allowed to sign in with your username. The modification will be shown, as depicted in the following screenshot:

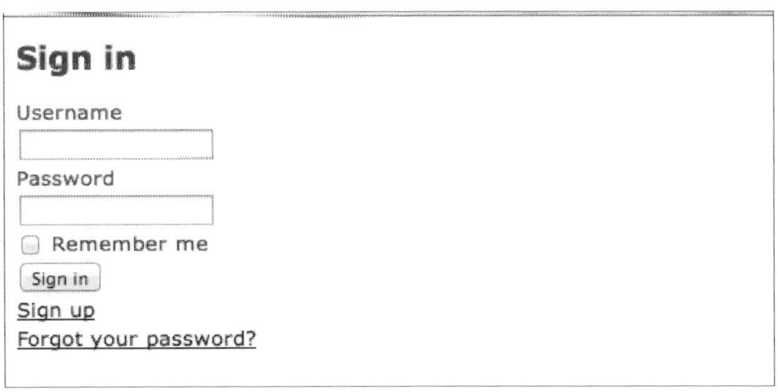

The sign-in page with username

- `app/views/devise/registrations/new.html.erb`: This file is a view file for the registration page. It is a bit different from the sign-up page; in this file, you need to add the `username` field, so that the user can fill in their username when they perform the registration.

```
#app/views/devise/registrations/new.html.erb

<h2>Sign Up</h2>

<%= form_for() do |f| %>
<%= devise_error_messages! %>

<div><%= f.label :email %><br />
<%= f.email_field :email, :autofocus => true %></div>

<div><%= f.label :username %><br />
<%= f.text_field :username %></div>

<div><%= f.label :password %><br />
<%= f.password_field :password %></div>

<div><%= f.label :password_confirmation %><br />
<%= f.password_field :password_confirmation %></div>

<div><%= f.submit "Sign up" %></div>
<% end %>

<%= render "devise/shared/links" %>
```

Especially for registration, you need to perform extra modifications. Previously, in *Chapter 1, Devise – Authentication Solution for Ruby on Rails*, we have talked about mass assignment rules written in the `app/controller/application_controller.rb` file, and now, we are going to modify them a little. Add `username` to the sanitizer for sign-in and sign-up, and you will have something as follows:

```
#these codes are written inside configure_permitted_parameters
function

devise_parameter_sanitizer.for(:sign_in) {|u| u.permit(:email,
:username)}
devise_parameter_sanitizer.for(:sign_up) {|u|
u.permit(:email, :username, :password, :password_confirmation)}
```

These changes will allow you to perform a sign-up along with the username data. The result of the preceding example is shown in the following screenshot:

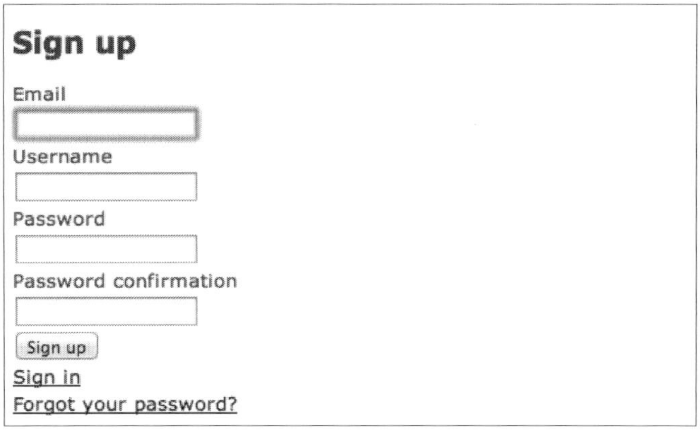

The sign-up page with username

I want to add a new case for your sign-in, which is only one field for username and e-mail. This means that you can sign in either with your e-mail ID or username like in Twitter's sign-in form. Based on what we have done before, you already have `username` and `email` columns; now, open `/app/models/user.rb` and add the following line:

```
attr_accessor :signin
```

Next, you need to change the authentication keys for Devise. Open `/config/initializers/devise.rb` and change the value for `config.authentication_keys`, as shown in the following code snippet:

```
config.authentication_keys = [ :signin ]
```

Let's go back to our user model. You have to override the lookup function that Devise uses when performing a sign-in. To do this, add the following method inside your `model` class:

```
def self.find_first_by_auth_conditions(warden_conditions)
    conditions = warden_conditions.dup
    where(conditions).where(["lower(username) = :value OR lower(email)
= :value", { :value => signin.downcase }]).first
end
```

As an addition, you can add a validation for your username, so it will be case insensitive. Add the following validation code into your user model:

```
validates :username, :uniqueness => {:case_sensitive => false}
```

Please open /app/controller/application_controller.rb and make sure you have this code to perform parameter filtering:

```
before_filter :configure_permitted_parameters, if: :devise_controller?

protected
  def configure_permitted_parameters
  devise_parameter_sanitizer.for(:sign_in) {|u| u.permit(:signin)}
  devise_parameter_sanitizer.for(:sign_up) {|u| u.permit(:email,
:username, :password, :password_confirmation)}
end
```

We're almost there! Currently, I assume that you've already stored an account that contains the e-mail ID and username. So, you just need to make a simple change in your sign-in view file (/app/views/devise/sessions/new.html.erb). Make sure that the file contains this code:

```
<h2>Sign in</h2>

<%= notice %>
<%= alert %>

<%= form_for(resource, :as => resource_name, :url => session_
path(resource_name)) do |f| %>
  <div><%= f.label "Username or Email" %><br />
  <%= f.text_field :signin, :autofocus => true %></div>

  <div><%= f.label :password %><br />
  <%= f.password_field :password %></div>

  <% if devise_mapping.rememberable? -%>
    <div><%= f.check_box :remember_me %> <%= f.label :remember_me %></
div>
  <% end -%>

  <div><%= f.submit "Sign in" %></div>
<% end %>

<%= render "devise/shared/links" %>
```

You can see that you don't have a username or email field anymore. The field is now replaced by a single field named :signin that will accept either the e-mail ID or the username. It's efficient, isn't it?

Updating the user account

Basically, you are already allowed to access your user account when you activate the **registerable** module in the model. To access the page, you need to log in first and then go to `/users/edit`. The page is as shown in the following screenshot:

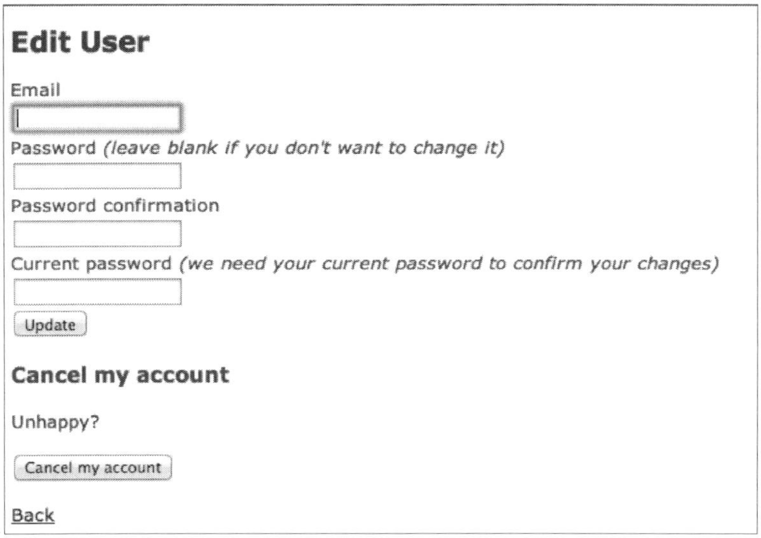

The edit account page

But, what if you want to edit your username or e-mail ID? How will you do that? What if you have extra information in your `users` table, such as addresses, birth dates, bios, and passwords as well? How will you edit these? Let me show you how to edit your user data including your password, or edit your user data without editing your password.

- **Editing your data, including the password**: To perform this action, the first thing that you need to do is modify your view. Your view should contain the following code:

  ```
  <div><%= f.label :username %><br />
  <%= f.text_field :username %></div>
  ```

  Now, we are going to overwrite Devise's logic. To do this, you have to create a new controller named `registrations_controller`. Please use the `rails` command to generate the controller, as shown:

  ```
  $ rails generate controller registrations update
  ```

It will produce a file located at app/controllers/. Open the file and make sure you write this code within the controller class:

```
class RegistrationsController < Devise::RegistrationsController
  def update
    new_params = params.require(:user).permit(:email,
    :username, :current_password, :password,
    :password_confirmation)

    @user = User.find(current_user.id)
    if @user.update_with_password(new_params)
      set_flash_message :notice, :updated
      sign_in @user, :bypass => true
      redirect_to after_update_path_for(@user)
    else
      render "edit"
    end
  end
end
```

Let's look at the code. Currently, Rails 4 has a new method in organizing whitelist attributes. Therefore, before performing mass assignment attributes, you have to prepare your data. This is done in the first line of the `update` method.

Now, if you see the code, there's a method defined by Devise named `update_with_password`. This method will use mass assignment attributes with the provided data. Since we have prepared it before we used it, it will be fine.

Next, you have to edit your route file a bit. You should modify the rule defined by Devise, so instead of using the original controller, Devise will use the controller you created before. The modification should look as follows:

```
devise_for :users, :controllers => {:registrations =>
"registrations"}
```

> **Downloading the example code**
>
> You can download the example code files for all Packt books you have purchased from your account at `http://www.packtpub.com`. If you purchased this book elsewhere, you can visit `http://www.packtpub.com/support` and register to have the files e-mailed directly to you.

Now you have modified the original user edit page, and it will be a little different. You can turn on your Rails server and see it in action. The view is as depicted in the following screenshot:

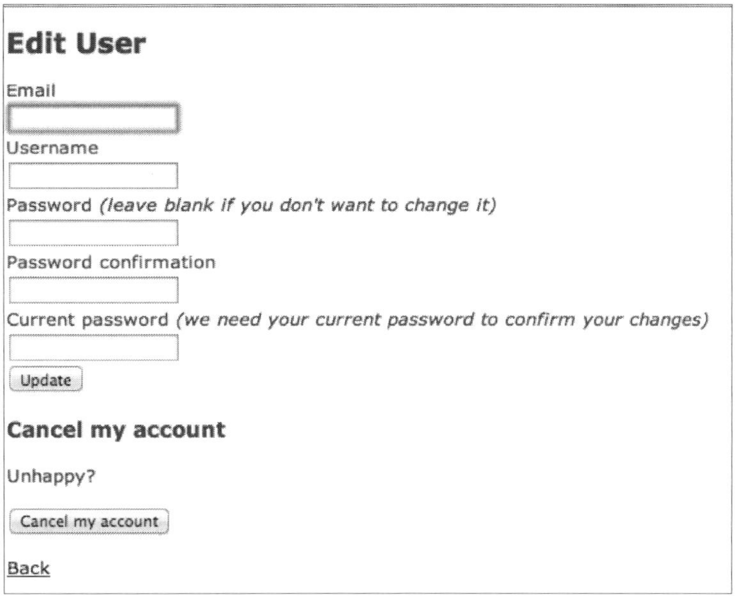

The modified account edit page

Now, try filling up these fields one by one. If you are filling them with different values, you will be updating all the data (e-mail, username, and password), and this sounds dangerous. You can modify the controller to have better data update security, and it all depends on your application's workflows and rules.

- **Editing your data, excluding the password**: Actually, you already have what it takes to update data without changing your password. All you need to do is modify your `registrations_controller.rb` file. Your `update` function should be as follows:

```
class RegistrationsController < Devise::RegistrationsController
  def update
    new_params = params.require(:user).permit(:email,
    :username, :current_password, :password,
    :password_confirmation)
    change_password = true
    if params[:user][:password].blank?
      params[:user].delete("password")
      params[:user].delete("password_confirmation")
```

```
      new_params = params.require(:user).permit(:email,
      :username)
      change_password = false
    end

    @user = User.find(current_user.id)
    is_valid = false

    if change_password
      is_valid = @user.update_with_password(new_params)
    else
      @user.update_without_password(new_params)
    end

    if is_valid
      set_flash_message :notice, :updated
      sign_in @user, :bypass => true
      redirect_to after_update_path_for(@user)
    else
      render "edit"
    end
  end
end
```

The main difference from the previous code is now you have an algorithm that will check whether the user intends to update your data with their password or not. If not, the code will call the `update_without_password` method. Now, you have codes that allow you to edit with/without a password. Now, refresh your browser and try editing with or without a password. It won't be a problem anymore.

Signing up the user with confirmation

Why does an application need to have an account confirmation? Actually, it's because the application needs the e-mail to be real, so that it can be used for future requirements. So, if one day you decide that you want to give a newsletter to your users periodically, you can consider applying this method to your application.

It's very simple to apply this method. You just need to activate the `:confirmable` module and have access to a mail server. The access is used to send a confirmation e-mail to the user, and for this example, I will show you how to use Gmail as your mail server.

You need to define the connection settings in your application. Because we are in the development environment, you can open the `config/environments/development.rb` file and add this code:

```
config.action_mailer.delivery_method = :smtp
config.action_mailer.perform_deliveries = true
config.action_mailer.raise_delivery_errors = true
config.action_mailer.smtp_settings = {
  :address => "smtp.gmail.com",
  :port => 587,
  :domain => "gmail.com",
  :user_name => <your_gmail_user_name>,
  :password => <your_gmail_password>,
  :authentication => 'plain',
  :enable_starttls_auto => true
}
```

Next, modify your `model` file and add a module, so your `model` file will be as follows:

```
class User < ActiveRecord::Base
    devise :database_authenticatable, :registerable, :recoverable,
    :rememberable, :trackable, :validatable, :confirmable
end
```

It's almost done. Now, create a migration file and modify it so that the content will be as follows:

```
class AddConfirmableToUsers < ActiveRecord::Migration
  def up
    add_column :users, :unconfirmed_email, :string
    add_column :users, :confirmation_token, :string
    add_column :users, :confirmed_at, :string
    add_column :users, :confirmation sent_at, :datetime

    add_index :users, :confirmation_token, :unique => true

    User.update_all(:confirmed_at => Time.now) #your current data
will be treated as if they have confirmed their account
  end

  def down
    remove_column :users, :unconfirmed_email,
    :confirmation_token, :confirmed_at, :confirmation_sent_at
  end
end
```

Execute the `rake db:migrate` command and your `users` table will be altered and ready to carry out the confirmation mechanism.

Now, run your Rails server and go to the registration page. Try registering a new account and see how it goes. Your application will send you an e-mail containing a link to confirm your account.

Resetting your password

"Oh my God! I forgot my password. How can I log in to the site?" It's very common that people forget the passwords of certain applications, and it will be a disaster if the application doesn't provide you with a feature to reset or create a new password. Resetting passwords has become a very important feature, and Devise provides it in an easy way.

To activate this module, your model should have the **recoverable** module in its Devise settings. Since this module requires a connection to an e-mail server, you will also need to define the configuration in order to establish a connection to a mail server. This can be done in the environment's configuration files as well. Fortunately, we don't need to worry because we have already met the requirement. So, you can directly go to your sign-in page and you will see a link labeled **Forgot your password?**. Click on it, fill in the **E-mail** field, and reset the password. In a moment, you will receive an e-mail sent by the Devise module. The e-mail will contain a link, which will bring you to a page, as shown in the following screenshot:

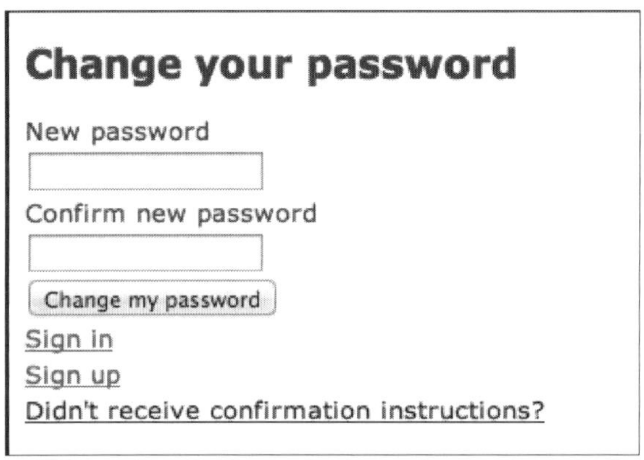

The change password page

Now, you can fill in your new password and submit it. Once you've submitted your new password, you'll be signed in again.

Canceling your account

Previously, we learned about how to update an account, register an account with a confirmation, and reset an account's password. Now, it's time for us to learn how to cancel an account.

This feature is provided to delete an account so that it won't be accessible anymore. By default, Devise provides this feature, and it can be accessed through the user edit page. As shown in the **Edit User** page, you can see a button labeled **Cancel my account**. If you press this button, Devise will delete your data from the database. So, if you want to access the application, you need to sign up again.

For some websites, data is like a treasure. Many websites don't perform deletions because they don't want to delete any data stored in their database. Instead of deleting it physically, the application will only change the flag of a data. Let's say, I have a user account that has a data flag, **published**. When I delete it, I don't delete the data but I change the flag of the data to **deleted**. But now, the question is how does Devise perform this method? Perform the following steps to know:

1. Create a migration file that will add a new column in the `users` table named `is_active` with the type, `integer`.
2. Add a method named `destroy` in `registration_controller.rb`, so it will contain the following code:

   ```
   def destroy
     @user = User.find(current_user.id)
     @user.is_active = 0
     if @user.save
       sign_out @user
       redirect_to root_path
     else
       render "edit"
     end
   end
   ```

3. Now, reload the user edit page and click on the **Cancel Account** button. You will be brought to the main page, but this time your data will not be deleted. It's now flagged with zero (**0**).

This is an example of many possibilities to be implemented as a replacement for data deletion. So, it depends on what you want to develop in your application.

Customizing Devise actions and routes

We have learned all the basic features that are commonly used in an application. Some of them are minimally customized and some of them are used as is. Maybe now is the time for you to wonder, "What if I want to customize Devise's actions, so that I can inject extra codes to do anything I want?" So, let's step forward to customize Devise's actions.

Technically, to perform action customizations, we need to create a controller that inherits Devise's controllers. It would be wise if you have a look at all of Devise's controllers first before we start this part, as shown at `https://github.com/plataformatec/devise/tree/master/app/controllers/devise`. So, when you start making some customizations, you will understand why you do it that way. However, I'm not going to tell you about the best practices of these customizations; I will only tell you the basics of performing the customizations. Therefore, what you will see in these examples are the instructions about what code you need to prepare and how you should access it.

- **Sign-up (registration)**: You can create a controller to override `registrations_controller.rb`, which contains the following code:

  ```
  class RegistrationsController < Devise::RegistrationController
    def new
      # this action is used to show the sign in form
      # you can add your custom code here
    end

    def create
      # this action is triggered when the user sends data to sign up
      # you can add your custom code here
    end
  end
  ```

  These two new methods will take effect if you change your route for Devise. Fortunately, we have modified the route file to comply with this customization. This is the route rule that is currently prevalent for Devise.

  ```
  devise_for :users, :controllers => {:registrations =>
  "registrations"}
  ```

  Now, you have the access to modify the action to meet your needs. You can write an extra process before or after the sign-up action. But, you need to remember that you have to write some code that already existed in the parent controller because without these codes your action won't work well. You can see the parent file at `https://github.com/plataformatec/devise/blob/master/app/controllers/devise/registrations_controller.rb`.

- **User edit**: To customize this action, you can continue editing `registrations_controller.rb` and adding these codes inside the class:

```
def edit
  # this action is used to show the user edit form page
  # you can add your custom code here
end

def update
  # this action is triggered when the user sends data to edit
their data
  # you can add your custom code here
end
```

  You don't need to make changes to your routes since you already made changes when you customized the user sign-up (registration) action.

- **Confirmation**: The first thing you need to do is create a controller file named `confirmations_controller.rb`. This file can be created by executing the following command:

```
$ rails generate controller confirmations new create
```

  The content of this newly-created controller is as follows:

```
class ConfirmationsController < Devise::ConfirmationsController
  def new
    # this action is used to show the confirmation form
    # you can add your custom code here
  end

  def create
    # this action is triggered when the user sends their
    confirmation token to confirm their account
     # you can add your custom code here
  end
end
```

  To make Devise recognize that you have overridden its original class, you also need to modify the routes for your Devise model. As an example, we will use the user model. Combined with the registration customization, the route will be as follows:

```
devise_for :users, :controllers => {:registrations =>
"registrations", :confirmations => "confirmations"}
```

- **User deletion**: To create a custom code for deleting a user, you also need to modify `registrations_controller.rb`. Put this method within the class:

  ```
  def destroy
      # this method is triggered when the user tries to delete a
  user account
  end
  ```

  You don't need to modify your routes anymore because the requirement is met when you customized the user sign-up (requirement) code.

- **Sign-in**: Execute the following command to create a controller named `sessions_controller.rb`:

  ```
  $ rails generate controller sessions new create
  ```

  The controller you just generated will contain this code:

  ```
  class SesssionsController < Devise::SessionsController
    def new
      # this method is used to show the sign in form
      # you can add your custom code here
    end

    def create
      # this method is triggered when the user sends data to sign in
      # you can add your custom code here
    end
  end
  ```

  To make Devise recognize your custom code, you have to modify your Devise route a little. Combined with the previous customizations, the route should be as follows:

  ```
  devise_for :users, :controllers => {:registrations =>
  "registrations", :confirmations => "confirmations", :sessions =>
  "sessions"}
  ```

- **Sign-out**: To customize this action, you need to modify `sessions_controller.rb`, which you just created. Please put the following method within the class:

  ```
  def destroy
    # this method is triggered when the user sends data to sign out
    # you can add your custom code here
  end
  ```

  You don't need to modify your routes since it has been done when you performed your code customization in the sign-in action.

- **Forgot password**: Please create a new controller file named `passwords_controller.rb`. You can do this by executing the following command:

  ```
  $ rails generate controller passwords new create
  ```

  The controller will contain this code:

  ```
  class PasswordsController < Devise::PasswordsController
    def new
      # this method will show a forgot password form
      # you can add your custom code here
    end

    def create
      # this method is triggered when you submit to reset your
  password
      # you can add your custom code here
    end
  end
  ```

Now, to enable your code customization, you have to modify your routes. Combined with the previous code customizations, your route should be like this:

```
devise_for :users, :controllers => {:registrations => "registrations",
:confirmations => "confirmations", :sessions => "sessions", :passwords
=> "passwords"}
```

Customizing your Devise layout

There are times when you have more than one Devise model in one application, and a question comes to your mind, such as "How do I maintain its views so that they will have different views?" Previously, I wrote about generating views, so you can make some custom changes to the views by executing the following command:

```
$ rails generate devise:views
```

Now, you are going to learn about how to generate scoped views in Devise. At first, you need to make a little modification to `config/initializers/devise.rb`. You need to remove the comment tag for this code:

```
config.scoped_views = true
```

This code will enable scoped views for Devise, so you can generate some specific views for your Devise model.

Before we start generating views, let's have two new Devise models for `admin` and `employee` as the examples. Now, you can generate scoped views for your Devise model by executing this command:

```
$ rails generate devise:views admins
$ rails generate devise:views employees
```

The following screenshot shows the generated Devise view files:

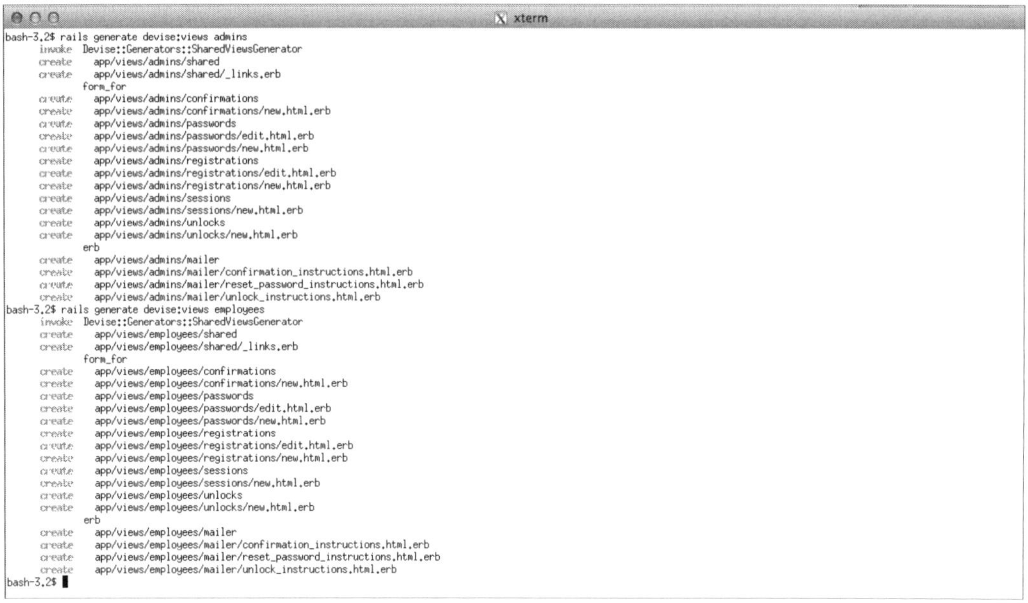

Let me show you how it works by making a simple change to each view file; for example, we are going to make changes in `app/views/admins/sessions/new.html.erb` and `app/views/employees/sessions/new.html.erb`. In my case, I put words such as "admins" and "employees" in `<h2>` tags in each file, so we can expect them to have different views when we open their sign-in form. I assume that you have the `admins` and `employees` controllers that define the `index` action. The action is authorized by `admin` and `employee`. Now, try starting the Rails server and go through `http://localhost:3000/employees/index.http://localhost:3000/employees/index`.

The sign-in form for an employee

You have seen the scoped image for an employee sign-in form; now you need to go through `http://localhost:3000/admins/indexhttp://localhost:3000/admins/index` and you will see the scoped view for an admin:

The sign-in form for an admin

You have successfully created different views for your Devise model, but you still have only one layout. So, how will you apply different layouts to different Devise models? Don't worry, it's actually easy to do that. Please open `app/controllers/application_controller.rb` and put this code within the class:

```
layout :layout_by_resource

protected
  def layout_by_resource
  if devise_controller?
    if resource_name == :admin
```

```
      "devise_admin_application" #admin model will use this layout
    elsif resource_name == :employee
      "devise_employee_application" #employee model will use this
layout
    else
      "devise_application" #other devise model will use this
layout
    end
  else
    "application" #default rails application layout
  end
end
```

Now, you need to create three new files under `app/view/layouts` named `devise_admin_application.html.erb`, `devise_employee_application.html.erb`, and `devise_application.html.erb`. Put anything you like as a mark to denote that you are in a different layout. If you go through the employee page, you will see a view, as shown in the following screenshot:

Specific layout for an employee

Now, try accessing the sign-in page for the admin model. You will find it different based on the mark you put in the layout for admin. In my case, the view is as shown in the following screenshot:

Specific layout for admin

If you have more than two Devise models, the other one will also have a different layout. In my case, I used a default layout, which is defined by `devise_application.html.erb`. The result is as shown in the following screenshot:

The default layout for a Devise model

Integrating Devise with Mongoid

This is an example of how you are able to implement Devise with one of the NoSQL databases, such as MongoDB. To establish a connection, we are going to use **Mongoid** as a driver. I'm going to show you two examples. The first example will require a fresh Rails application where you need to generate a new Rails application, and the second one will show you how to change the configuration from MySQL to MongoDB. Note that these examples will use MongoDB Version 2.2.0 and I will not tell you how to install MongoDB, but you can see the full documentation about its installation at `http://docs.mongodb.org/manual/installation/`. As you can see in the documentation, it also shows you how to turn on the server; therefore, I assume you have done it before you proceed to the next step.

Now, we can start from the first example by executing the Rails application generation command without specifying the database type:

```
$ rails new learning-devise-mongoid
```

Next, you need to add two new gems inside `Gemfile` and after you have added them, you can install them by executing `bundle install`:

```
gem 'mongoid'
gem 'devise'
```

Now, you need to create a configuration file for Mongoid by executing the following command:

```
$ rails generate mongoid:config
```

In my case, I don't need to change anything in my Mongoid configuration. But, if you want to see the content of the configuration file or you need to change something in it, you can open the file at `config/mongoid.yml`.

Since we are no longer using active record, we need to modify the `config/application.rb` file and remove the line, `require 'rails/all'`, while adding this code:

```
require 'action_controller/railtie'
require 'action_mailer/railtie'
require 'rails/test_unit/railtie'
require 'sprockets/railtie'
```

You also need to modify one of the files in `config/environments`; for this example, we are going to modify `development.rb` because we are currently in the development environment. Please remove or comment out this line of code:

```
config.active_record.migration_error = :page_load
```

The configuration for Mongoid is done; now, we are going to move to the Devise configuration. There is no difference in setting up Devise with Mongoid; the commands and steps that you need to perform are exactly the same with the ones that I've written in the previous chapter. But, there's one difference in the Devise configuration file. If you open config/initializers/devise.rb, usually you are going to see the require 'devise/orm/active_record' line inside it. But, if you use Devise with Mongoid, you are going to see that the code will be replaced with the following code:

```
require 'devise/orm/mongoid'
```

Let's say I generated a user Devise model and I also generated a users controller to see whether it's working or not. My controller will be like this:

```
class UsersController < ApplicationController
  before_filter :authenticate_user!
  def index
  end
end
```

These will be the codes for my view:

```
<h1>Users#index</h1>
<p>Find me in app/views/users/index.html.erb</p>
<%= link_to 'Sign Out', destroy_user_session_path, method: "delete" %>
```

When you go through http://localhost:3000/users/indexhttp://localhost:3000/users/index, you are going to be redirected to the following page:

The Devise sign-in form with Mongoid

Your Devise is installed and ready to use. If you want to determine whether your data is recorded or not in your MongoDB, you can try the commands shown in the following screenshot:

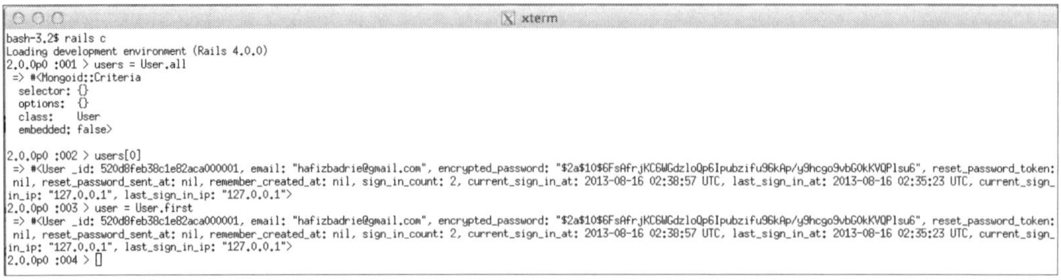

Commands in the Rails console to check MongoDB data

What if you already have the Rails application installed with the `mysql2` gem and suddenly you decide to change your database to MongoDB? Don't worry. You don't need to regenerate your Rails application from scratch. You just need to follow the steps that I'm going to put before you. But, I assume that you are going to start the application from a brand new database, so your existing user data will be abandoned.

First of all, you need to modify `Gemfile` by replacing the line, `gem 'mysql2'`, with `gem 'mongoid', git: 'https://github.com/mongoid/mongoid.git'`. The next step is to modify `config/application.rb` so that the file will contain the following code:

```
#require 'rails/all' #you don't need this line anymore
require "action_controller/railtie"
require "action_mailer/railtie"
require "rails/test_unit/railtie"
require "sprockets/railtie"
```

Now, you need to modify `config/environments/development.rb` by commenting out the following line:

```
#config.active_record.migration_error = :page_load
```

These are the basic configurations that you need to perform before generating the Mongoid configuration with this command:

```
$ rails generate mongoid:config
```

Don't forget to open `config/initializers/devise.rb` and modify it as shown:

```
#require 'devise/orm/active_record'
require 'devise/orm/mongoid
```

All set! Now, you can go to the authorized page and see the Devise sign-in form. Don't forget that you don't have the previous data in MySQL in your MongoDB; consequently, you need to re-register your user data.

Summary

Now, I believe that you will be able to make your own Rails application with Devise. You should be able to make your own customizations based on your needs. You will have a more comprehensive understanding about Devise modules and how you should make your own customizations either in the logic flow or the view codes. Next, we will learn how to implement privileges in Devise because in some circumstances, privileges will be needed to prevent certain users from accessing some features. Everything about privileges in Devise will be discussed in the next chapter.

3
Privileges

In the previous chapter, you learned how to use Devise authentication features such as user session and registration management (sign-in, sign-up, sign-out, and so on).

After users are logged in, you will want to make sure that they can only access pages and page elements that they are supposed to see. You will want to define access control rules or privileges so that users cannot see protected resources, such as other users' private posts. The process of applying the rules in our web application is called **authorization**.

In Rails apps, the **CanCan gem** (`https://github.com/ryanb/cancan`) can be used for authorization by defining and applying privileges of what users can or cannot do. At the same time, Devise will still be used for authentication.

Let's take an example web application that uses CanCan together with Devise. After that, we will discuss more details on using CanCan, as well as testing and debugging it.

CollabBlogs – a web application for collaborative writing

Imagine that we are going to build a Rails web application that facilitates collaborative writing. Let's call it CollabBlogs. Assume that its basic functionalities are as follows:

- Guest users (not logged-in users) can read non-restricted posts.
- Only logged-in users can create posts.
- An administrator user can do anything he/she wants.
- A user can delete his/her own posts; he/she cannot delete posts created by other users.

- A restricted post is a post that can be viewed by its creator and the collaborators chosen by him/her. If there is no collaborator, only the creator can see the restricted post.
- Many users can edit a post, if the post creator chooses to collaborate with them.

We are not going to implement all of them; we will only implement the essential ones together. The rest are left as exercises for you.

Before we try out CanCan, let's do some initial setup:

1. Make sure you finished setting up Devise by following the instructions given in the previous chapter.
2. Add `gem 'cancan', '~>1.6.0'` to your `Gemfile`.
3. Run the `bundle` command in your terminal.
4. Add the Boolean `admin` column on `user`.
5. Create a **scaffold** for `Post` and a **model** for `Collaboration`, and then, run the migrations. The scaffold will create JSON views, which will not be discussed in this book. You are free to add your own model validations before running the migrations.

   On your terminal, run the following commands:

   ```
   $> rails g scaffold post user:references title content:text restricted:boolean
   $> rails g model collaboration user:references post:references
   $> rake db:migrate
   ```

   After that, make sure that the `Post` class `belongs_to :user` and `has_many :collaborations`

6. Create a few users and posts, as many as you like. For example, in your Rails console (or `db/seeds.rb`):

   ```
   writer = User.find_or_create_by!(email: "writer@localhost.net",
   password: "Plumber364", password_confirmation: "Plumber364")
   junior = User.find_or_create_by!(email: "junior@localhost.net",
   password: "Plumber364", password_confirmation: "Plumber364")

   Post.create!(user: writer, title: "Hot Day",
     content: "The sun seems to like me very much these days. I don't
   really mind, but I really wish it could love someone else too.")
   Post.create!(user: junior, title: "Hello!",
   ```

```
  content: "Hey! I'm pretty new here! Glad to be here! This is my
first time here, so please be nice to me (and each other).")
```

Once our web application structure is adequately prepared, we'll pick a simple rule to implement: **A user can delete his/her own posts; he/she cannot delete posts created by other users**. The following four fundamental steps will make CanCan handle authorization work for you.

7. Defining authorization rules: All privilege rules reside in `ability.rb`, which is placed under `app/models`. Run `rails g cancan:ability` so that Rails generates `ability.rb` for you. CanCan provides you with `can` and `cannot` methods for defining access controls. Let's take a look at an example:

```
# app/models/ability.rb
class Ability
  include CanCan::Ability

  def initialize(user)
    if user && user.persisted? # Logged-in user
      # User can destroy his/her own post
      can :destroy, Post, user_id: user.id

      # Non-logged in users cannot destroy Posts.
      # Typically, can is used a lot more than cannot.
      # cannot :destroy, Post, user_id: nil
    end
  end
end
```

As we have seen, the `can` and `cannot` methods take three arguments: action name, the resource class, and a hash of rule conditions. Although the arguments seem restrictive, the methods can actually accept different kinds of arguments such as SQL conditions and blocks. We will discuss this in detail in a later section.

8. Restricting views based on the rules: Now that we have the access rules, we can apply them in views. CanCan comes with view helpers (`can?` and `cannot?`) to check authorization in views.

```
<%# app/views/posts/index.html.erb %>
<% if can?(:destroy, post) %>
  <%= link_to('Del', post, class: 'btn-gray thinner-padding',
method: :delete, data: { confirm: 'Are you sure?' }) %>
<% end %>
```

```
<%# using cannot? %>
<%# Typically, can? is used a lot more than cannot? %>

<% if cannot?(:destroy, post) %>
  <p>It looks like you cannot delete this post. If you want this
post to be deleted, please contact the administrator or the
owner.</p>
<% end %>
```

Run the Rails server by executing `rails s` in your terminal, and open `http://localhost:3000` in your browser to see if the destroy link is visible for logged-in users, the post creator, or guest users.

9. Restricting controller access based on the defined rules: You restricted views accordingly, and you noticed that someone could just use the URL (via CURL, for example) to delete the post. This leads to the need of authorization check controllers.

   CanCan provides a few authorization-related methods in controllers. One of the most frequently used methods is `authorize!`, which accepts two arguments, an action name, and a resource. The method raises the `CanCan::AccessDenied` exception when the currently logged-in user's privileges are not enough to perform the action on the resource.

   For example, we can check for a current user's privileges on creating a new post and destroying an existing post as follows:

```
class PostsController < ApplicationController
  before_action :set_post, only: [:show, :edit,
    :update, :destroy]
  # ...

  def new
    authorize! :new, Post
    # codes for new...
  end
  # ...

  def destroy
    authorize! :destroy, @post
    @post.destroy
    # ...
  end
end
```

You might find this way tedious, especially if you need to authorize every controller action. We will discuss a way to simplify this in a later section.

10. Customizing the response for unauthorized access: Great! You ensured that users could only delete their own posts. When an unprivileged user (an anonymous visitor, for example) tries to delete another user's post, he/she will get the default 403 forbidden error page. This is because CanCan raises the `CanCan::AccessDenied` exception whenever an unauthorized user tries to access any restricted controller action.

    In some cases, you need to customize the look and feel of the forbidden page. Feel free to do so by rescuing from `CanCan::AccessDenied` and rendering a custom view.

    ```
    # app/controllers/application_controller.rb
    class ApplicationController < ActionController::Base
      rescue_from CanCan::AccessDenied do |exception|
        if current_user.nil? # user is not logged in
          session[:next] = request.fullpath
          redirect_to login_url,
            :alert => "Please log in to continue."
        else
          if request.env["HTTP_REFERER"].present?
            redirect_to :back, :alert => exception.message
          else
            render :file => "#{Rails.root}/public/403.html",
              :status => 403, :layout => false
          end
        end
      end
    # ...
    end
    ```

With custom CSS and JavaScript we have in our sample project, we can have a list of posts displayed with actions allowed for the visitors, like the following:

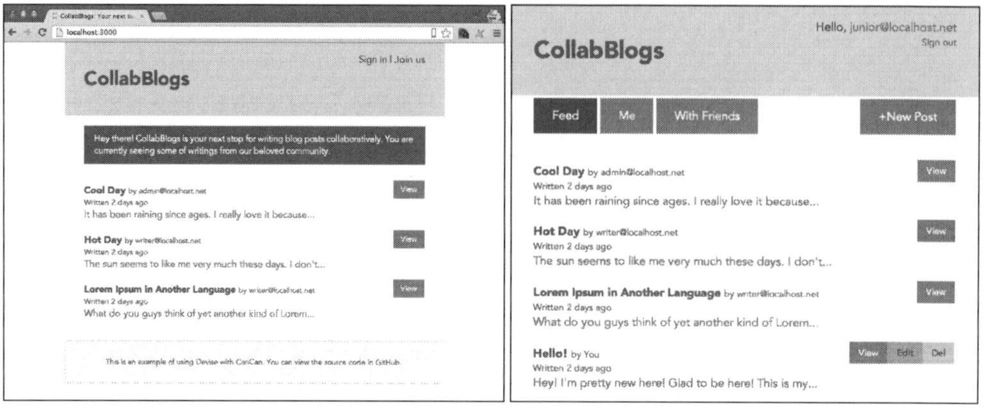

Screenshots of a guest user's page (left) and a logged-in user's page (right)

Advanced CanCan usages

The previous abilities we learned through our CollabBlogs application are enough for us to get started. However, what if our application requires complex authorization rules? We have a few remaining complex rules unimplemented, and the abilities we have applied are far simpler than those complex rules.

After we have plenty of rules, we should try to simplify parts of the authorization process and test the rules' correctness. This is to ensure our application behaves as expected.

In this section, we are going to discuss defining rules using SQL, simplifying authorization checks on controllers, and ensuring abilities' correctness.

Defining rules using SQL

As mentioned before, the `can` and `cannot` methods we defined in `app/models/abilities.rb`, are able to take SQL conditions and block parameters. The SQL conditions parameter is useful for filtering resources that match the ability (using `Model#accessible_by(ability, action)`). The block parameter is very often used for authorizing actions (for example, edit) on a single resource.

As a small example, let's use these parameters on the `destroy` abilities we have defined, as shown in the following code snippet:

```
# We can write
can :destroy, Post, user_id: user.id
# as a new rule that looks similar
can :destroy, Post, ['user_id = ?', user.id]
```

> Note that the new rule is not quite the same as the old one; the SQL query will only help build queries using the CanCan model scope `Model#accessible_by(ability, action)`; it will not work if/when you apply the rule on your views.

To make it work on views, implement a block that looks equivalent to the SQL. CanCan will use the block when you apply checks on the views. So, the correct block-based definition for the earlier rule is as follows:

```
can :destroy, Post, ['user_id = ?', user.id] do |post|
  post.user_id == user.id
end
```

The block is evaluated when an instance of post is passed for checking. You should not do something, as shown in the following snippet:

```
# Admin can do anything
can :manage, :all do |post|
  user.admin?
end
```

In some cases, for instance, when you try to check a user's ability to create a new post using `can?(:create, Post)`, the block above will not get called. Such behavior potentially breaks your application. Instead, the correct way is as follows:

```
if user.admin?
  can :manage, :all # An administrator can do anything
else
  # Regular user
end
```

Now that we know how to use SQL conditions and blocks to implement abilities, let's try to use them for abilities that require SQL subselects, as shown in the following sections.

> A restricted post is a post that can be viewed by the creator and the collaborators chosen by the creator. If there is no collaborator, only the creator can see the post.

We can break down the preceding rules to the following three conditions:

- Non-restricted posts are viewable by anyone
- Posts created by the currently logged-in user are viewable
- If a post is restricted, only the post' collaborators and creator can view it

From these three rules, we can see that they are related to the `index` and `show` actions in `PostsController`. We will pass an array of the `:index` and `:show` actions to the `can` method, because it takes an array of actions as the first argument, instead of just one action.

```
# the above rules for logged-in users
indexable_condition = <<-EOC
restricted = ? OR posts.user_id = ? OR
  (restricted = ? AND EXISTS
    (SELECT * FROM collaborations WHERE
      collaborations.post_id = posts.id AND
      collaborations.user_id = ?))
EOC

can [:index, :show], Post, [indexable_condition,
  false, user.id, true, user.id] do |post|
  !post.restricted? || post.user_id == user.id ||
    (post.restricted? &&
     post.collaborations.where(
       user_id: user.id).present?)
end
```

Although this way of using the CanCan ability is not the best way, it shows how you can leverage CanCan abilities to express complex SQL-based rules.

To display the list of posts that match the currently logged-in user's ability in the `index` action of `PostsController`, assign `Post.accessible_by(current_ability, :index)` to `@posts` instead of assigning `Post.all`.

With custom JS and CSS provided in the sample project, we can see a list of posts that are viewable by the currently logged-in user like this. Note that we can apply view checks on each of the buttons shown (**View**, **Edit**, and **Delete**).

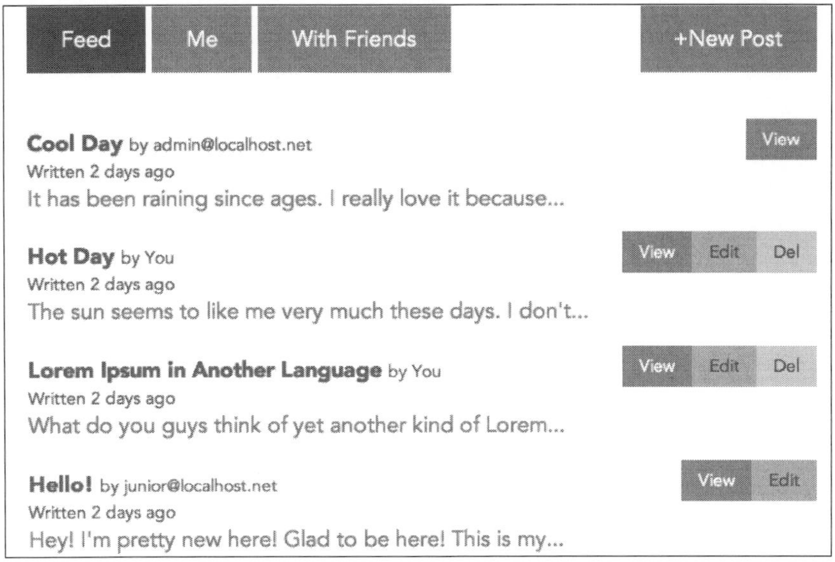

A screenshot of a page of a logged-in user who can edit another user's post

How about the rest of the rules? Feel free to try implementing them yourself!

Simplifying authorization checks on controllers

You can also use `authorize_resource` so that CanCan authorizes every controller action as in the following example. This is as an alternative to calling `authorize_resources!` on every controller action:

```
class PostsController < ApplicationController
  before_action :set_post, only: [:show, :edit,
    :update, :destroy]
  authorize_resource
  def new
    # authorization check is done
  end
  # ...
  def destroy
    # authorization check is done
  end
end
```

Ensuring abilities' correctness

Our application will get big and challenging to maintain. When we have lots of rules, we need to make sure they work as expected. Luckily, CanCan makes testing and debugging privileges delightful.

Testing

Testing abilities can be done using several test frameworks such as **Test::Unit**, **RSpec**, and **Cucumber**. In this section, we will use RSpec for testing abilities.

CanCan provides an **RSpec** matcher (`be_able_to`) to make it convenient to test abilities:

```
# specs/models/ability_spec.rb
require "cancan/matchers"
require "spec_helper"

describe Ability do
  describe "destroying a post" do
    describe "guest user" do
      let(:ability) { Ability.new nil }

      it "cannot destroy a post" do
        ability.should_not be_able_to(
          :destroy, Post.new(user: nil))
        ability.should_not be_able_to(
          :destroy, Post.new)
      end
    end
  end
end
```

Debugging

You can debug the defined abilities in a Rails console, during test or during development. In general, the following are the steps to debug abilities:

1. Fetch a user and a model you would like to debug using the following code snippet:

   ```
   user = User.first # a user you want to check
   post = Post.first # a model you want to check
   ability = Ability.new(user)
   ```

2. Check if the ability behaves correctly for those records. Use the model scope to verify if the defined abilities filter the correct records.

```
# behavior checks
puts ability.can?(:edit, post)
puts ability.can?(:create, Post)

# the accessible records on index action
Post.accessible_by(ability, :index)

# the SQL query
puts Post.accessible_by(ability, :index).to_sql
```

Summary

In this chapter, we discussed setting up a Rails project that used CanCan for authorizing user abilities. We learned how to define authorization rules using CanCan abilities, how to apply rules on views using CanCan view helpers, and how to authorize controllers based on the defined rules. Finally, we saw how to ensure the correctness of defined rules.

4

Remote Authentication with Devise and OmniAuth

By following footpaths from the previous chapters, we will be able to create an application that authenticates its users using their supplied e-mail addresses and passwords. However, the e-mail address and password authentication is not the only way that can be used to verify a user's credential; there are actually several other alternatives that we can choose from. One such example that is now widely used is **remote authentication**.

Remote authentication

Have you seen buttons similar to the buttons in this following screenshot on websites that you have visited? The sign-in process that is initiated by clicking on these will actually trigger a remote authentication procedure:

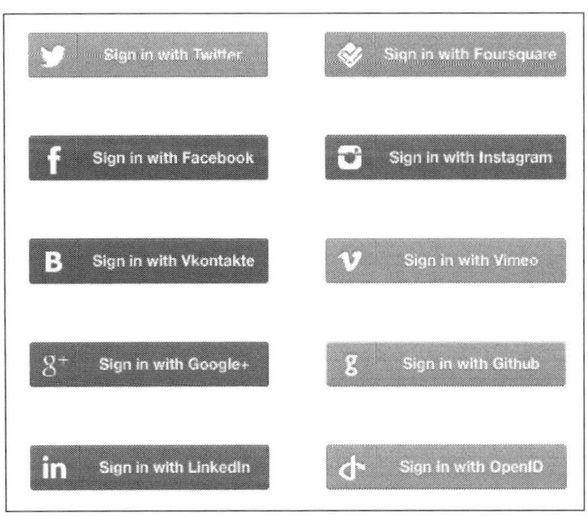

Remote authentication is an authentication scheme that utilizes third-party services to help identify whether a user, who tries to log in, has valid credentials prior to entering an authenticated area. By using this scheme to authenticate, users just have to sign in once with third-party providers that provide such services, and then they can sign in to other websites that support remote authentication without supplying their e-mail addresses and passwords anymore.

Popular websites, such as Twitter, Facebook, and even Google, provide remote authentication services to its users. Surely, due to the huge number of users, it would be good if our websites could authenticate its users using only their Twitter, Facebook, or Google accounts.

At this point perhaps you're wondering why big companies like them want to act as remote authentication providers who give authentication services to other websites for free. Isn't that a waste of their bandwidth and resources? That question of course has its own merits. Remote authentication providers won't usually give these services to just anyone. To utilize it, we have to first register our application at their site. This is to ensure that they can track every application that use their services and can provide assistance in case of trouble. They also have the right to reject or ban our application if we misuse or violate their term of rights.

Meanwhile, providing these services also has benefits for them; remember that users have to register a new account at their site before they can authenticate using it? That's an important benefit for them. By providing these services, remote authentication providers can increase their user base.

OmniAuth

Let's now take a closer look at Devise and how it can support remote authentication. By itself, Devise is already customizable enough to enable support for remote authentication. However, Devise doesn't actually have internal functions for this purpose, and as a consequence, we have to do a lot of lifting to build this feature purely using Devise. Therefore, because it is almost always better to "re-use" rather than "build from scratch", let's look into other possible alternatives.

Enter **OmniAuth** (`https://github.com/intridea/omniauth`). If you remember from *Chapter 1, Devise – Authentication Solution for Ruby on Rails*, Devise has an `Omniauthable` module that enables Devise to connect with OmniAuth; this is where you will find that ability useful.

> "*OmniAuth is a library that standardizes* **multiprovider authentication** *for web applications. It was created to be* **powerful**, **flexible**, *and* **do as little as possible**. *Any developer can create strategies for OmniAuth that can authenticate users via* **disparate systems**. *OmniAuth strategies have been created for* **everything** *from* **Facebook** *to* **LDAP**."

Based on the preceding description by OmniAuth's author (present on the OmniAuth GitHub page), it was clear that OmniAuth is the library that we want. First, it enables support for multiprovider authentication. Second, it is flexible and we can create custom strategies if for some reason OmniAuth hasn't already provided support for providers that we want. Third, it already supports many providers; some of the most widely used providers, such as Twitter and Facebook, are already on that list. Therefore, we don't have to manually create an authentication strategy for Twitter and Facebook anymore. Perfect!

Implementing remote authentication in our application

Now, let's move on to the main part, where we will modify our previously created application so that it can support remote authentication. This section will be divided into several subsections. The following subsection will discuss the initial preparation, while the following two after that will discuss implementing Twitter and Facebook authentication consecutively. They are selected because they are currently reigning as providers with the most numbers of registered users.

Preparing your application

To enable OmniAuth on our applications, which already have Devise on them, we have to first include the OmniAuth gem by modifying our Gemfile. While we're at it, we can also include gems that contain OmniAuth strategies for both Twitter (`https://github.com/arunagw/omniauth-twitter`) and Facebook (`https://github.com/mkdynamic/omniauth-facebook`) to enable support for both providers.

```
...
# OmniAuth
gem 'omniauth', '~> 1.1.4'
gem 'omniauth-twitter', '~> 1.0.0'
gem 'omniauth-facebook', '~> 1.4.1'
...
```

If you use bundler, you may now call `bundle install` before continuing, so that Rails properly includes those new gems that were previously listed in our application.

After successfully including the OmniAuth gem in our application, we have to instruct Devise to activate the `omniauthable` module. We can do this by specifying it when initializing Devise on our `User` model (or any other model that you use that utilizes Devise).

```
devise :database_authenticatable, :registerable, :omniauthable,
:recoverable, :rememberable, :trackable, :validatable
```

Remote authentication using Twitter

Following successful initial configurations of our application, let us continue by adding the Twitter remote authentication support. To accomplish this, there are a few steps that we have to do. First, we will have to register our application at the Twitter developer site, which will be explained in the following subsection.

Registering our application at the Twitter developer site

We can head on straight to the Twitter developer site to register our application (`https://dev.twitter.com`). On entering the site, we will be greeted by information about various services that Twitter shares with third-party developers. We can sign in with our Twitter account to access the dashboard. However, if we don't have one, we must create a new Twitter account before continuing.

After a successful sign-in, we will find a pop-up menu in the top-right corner; you can click on **My applications** to enter the dashboard:

At the dashboard we can see all of our previously registered applications (if any). Click on **Create a new application** to register your application:

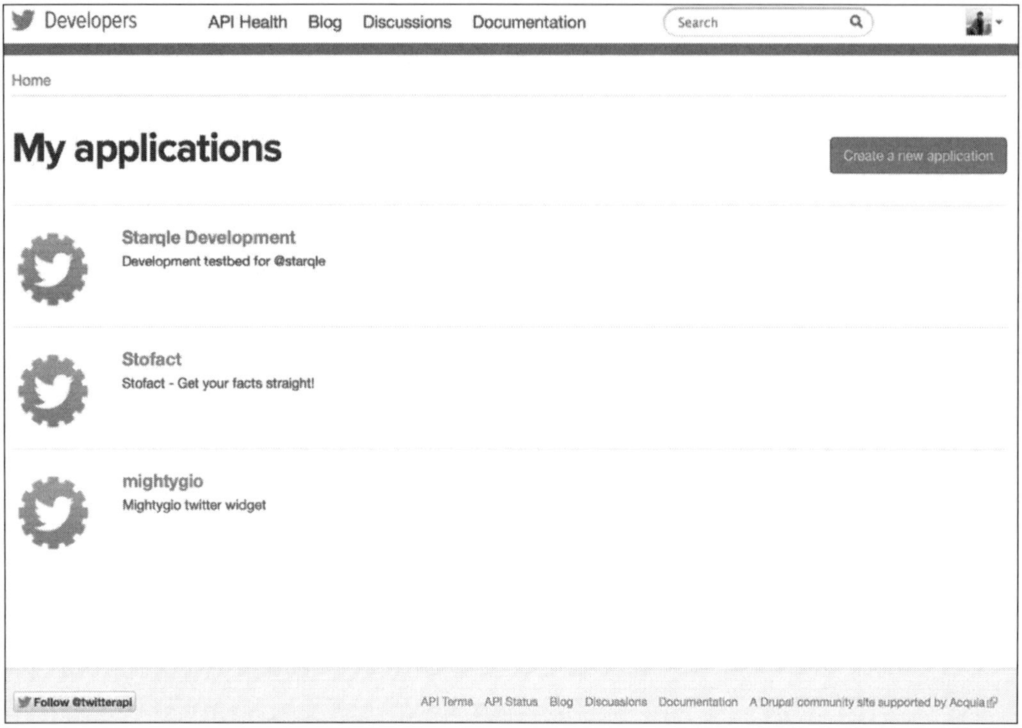

We will see a form that we have to fill in. There are four fields in this form, the first two are quite obvious (**Name** and **Description**), but we have to ensure the next two fields are entered correctly. In the **Website** field, we have to fill in a fully-qualified URL to our application. Because we're now registering an application for learning purposes and we don't actually have a real domain, we can put `localhost` into this field. However, as Twitter needs a fully-qualified URL, we have to type in `http://127.0.0.1:3000` instead of `http://localhost:3000`.

The last field is a bit tricky; this is a **Callback URL** field. Twitter will redirect into the URL that was specified here after a successful authentication. However, we can supply a custom parameter (`oauth_callback`) later from our application during the authentication process to override the value that was supplied to this field. Interestingly, the Devise and OmniAuth combination will automatically supply the `oauth_callback` parameter with our application URL followed by `/auth/:provider/callback`. Therefore, any value that we specified in this field won't matter much, as it would be overridden anyway. So, let's just fill this with a fully-qualified localhost URL where our application currently resides (the same with the website URL):

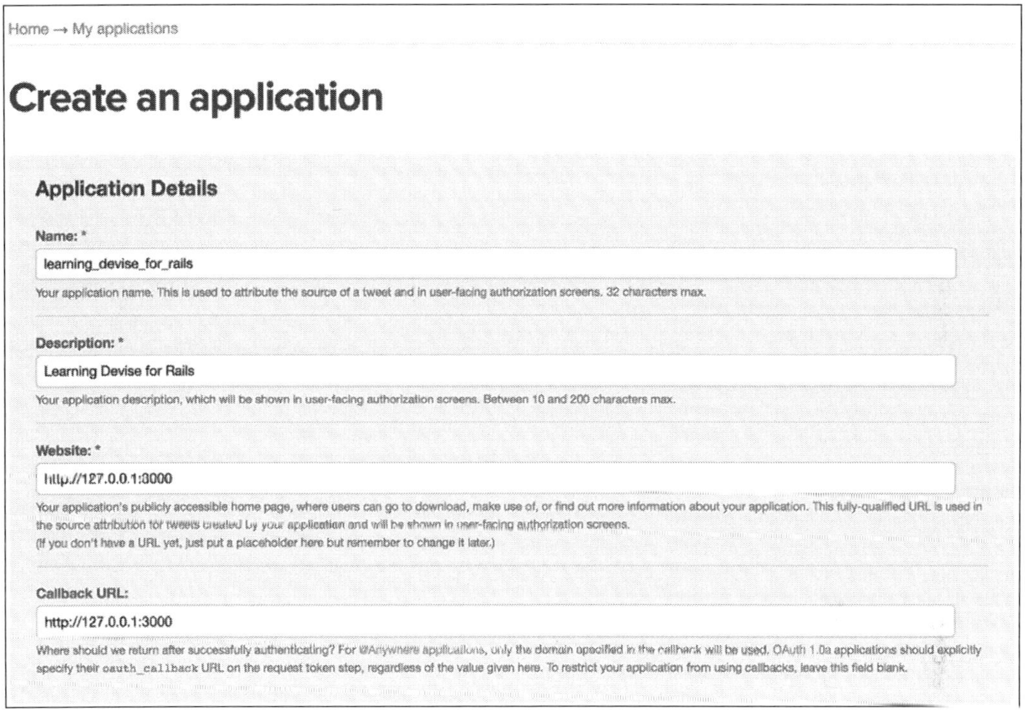

After you have finished filling in the form, we can submit it and Twitter will show the dashboard for our newly-created application. In this screen, we must write down both **Consumer key** and **Consumer secret** values because we will use it later in our application configuration. Both keys are important in helping our application identify itself to Twitter.

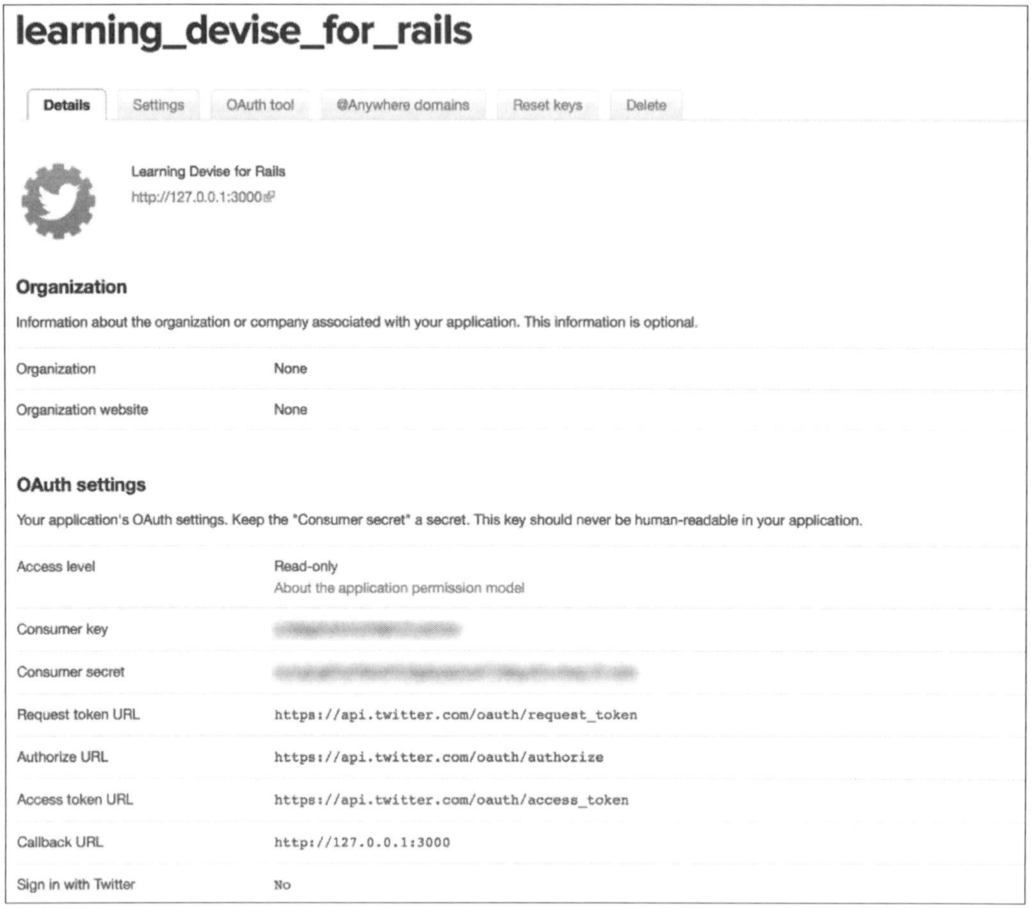

Configuring OmniAuth for authentication using Twitter

After successfully registering our application in the Twitter developer website, we can now set up our application to enable remote authentication using Twitter. We will begin by specifying the **Consumer key** and **Consumer secret** values that we got earlier from Twitter at `config/initializers/devise.rb`. We specify the configuration at the Devise initializer instead of OmniAuth because Devise will be the bridge that connects OmniAuth and our application.

Just to remind you, the consumer key and the consumer secret are our application's "username"' and "password" for Twitter's remote authentication, respectively. It is very important to keep both keys safe.

```
config.omniauth :twitter, 'CONSUMER_KEY', 'CONSUMER_SECRET'
```

> Remember that changes in any file within the `config/initializers` folder require an application restart. Don't forget to restart your application server after modifying Devise initializers.

By specifying the preceding configuration, Devise will also generate helpers for linking to the Twitter authentication, `user_omniauth_authorize_path(:twitter)`. This is assuming our model name that utilizes Devise is called `User`; if you use any other name, the helper will change accordingly. We can use the helpers in our home page or sign-in page like this:

```
<%= link_to "Sign in with Twitter", user_omniauth_authorize_
path(:twitter) %>
```

When users click on the link that was generated by the previously mentioned helper, they will be greeted by the Twitter application authorization page. This will only happen during their first visit; subsequent visits will instantly redirect back to our application after Twitter finishes authenticating our credentials. At the application authorization page, they will have to either authorize our application, or reject, in which case, they won't be able to sign in.

Up until this point, if we try to sign in using Twitter in our application and we choose to authorize it in the Twitter application authorization page, we will be redirected back but will see a "route does not exist" error page. This is normal because we haven't prepared appropriate routes, controllers, and views to handle the redirection.

Let's create it by using the Rails generator command (abbreviated `g`).

```
$ rails g controller omniauth_callbacks
```

Now, we have to tell Devise that the newly-generated controller will be the one that handles callbacks. To do that we can modify the existing `devise_for` routes by following the syntax in the following example:

```
devise_for :users, controllers: {omniauth_callbacks: "omniauth_
callbacks"}
```

Devise will automatically generate routes that link the callback URL of our application (the URL that will be supplied to the `oauth_callback` parameter) with a controller that will handle the callback logic. You can see the generated routes as follows:

```
user_omniauth_authorize GET|POST /users/auth/:provider(.:format)
omniauth_callbacks#passthru {:provider=>/twitter|facebook/}

user_omniauth_callback GET|POST /users/auth/:action/callback(.:format)
omniauth_callbacks#(?-mix:twitter|facebook)
```

The next step, is to modify OmniAuth callbacks that have been generated earlier. Devise has a class that we can inherit from; it's called `Devise::OmniauthCallbacksController`. So, let's inherit from it and specify our first action, `twitter`.

```
class OmniauthCallbacksController < Devise::OmniauthCallbacksControll
er
  def twitter
  end
end
```

Do you remember that users will be redirected back to our application after they authorize it in the Twitter authorization page? During the redirection, Twitter will actually supply extra information that we can parse and utilize for our sign-in process. This information is retrieved, processed, and stored by OmniAuth within the `request.env` hash using `omniauth.auth` as the key.

Let's inspect it by raising it in our callbacks controller.

```
class OmniauthCallbacksController < Devise::OmniauthCallbacksControll
er
  def twitter
    raise request.env["omniauth.auth"].to_yaml
  end
end
```

After specifying the raise, try to raise it by clicking on the sign-in using the Twitter link and authorize your application in the Twitter authorization page. We will see an exception page that shows all the authentication information that was given by Twitter.

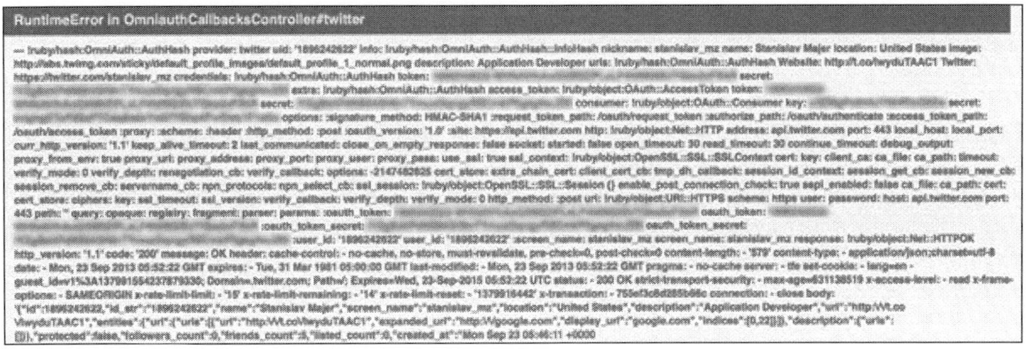

Rather than writing all the extra logic necessary for processing the information from the hash in the controller, it is better to delegate it into a class method to make the logic reusable and to keep our controller lean. Let's name the method `process_omniauth` and call it from our controller using the following code:

```
class OmniauthCallbacksController < Devise::OmniauthCallbacksControll
er
  def twitter
    user = User.process_omniauth(request.env["omniauth.auth"])
  end
end
```

When using the database authentication scheme, users will have to supply their username and password for authentication. This is not the case in a remote authentication scheme, because the third-party service will be the one that helps us in authenticating our users. Unfortunately, if we previously had a username and/or e-mail as the user's unique identifier in our database, our users won't be supplying that anymore. Instead, we have to look for other alternatives as the unique identifier. Luckily, Twitter supplies a `uid` value, which contains the unique user identifier that we can use.

We will store `uid` in our database within columns called `uid`. We will also store the provider name to indicate which authentication provider our users use in a column called `provider`. Let's create a migration for these new additions using the following commands:

```
$ rails g migration add_omniauth_to_users provider:string uid:string
$ rake db:migrate
```

> This scheme that we are building now assumes that one user can only choose one remote authentication provider to use, whether Twitter, Facebook, or Google. They cannot sign into the same account using more than one provider. See the summary at the end of this chapter for more information.

Next, let's create the `process_omniauth` method in our `User` model. We have been supplied with a hash as an argument that contains `provider` and `uid` information. Therefore, let's use this information to traverse our database and find whether a user with the `provider` and `uid` combination already exists:

```
def self.process_omniauth(auth)
  where(auth.slice(:provider, :uid)).first_or_create do |user|
    user.provider = auth.provider
    user.uid = auth.uid
    user.username = auth.info.nickname
  end
end
```

The most interesting part with the preceding code is the `first_or_create` method that we call. This is a method that was provided by `ActiveRecord`, which is a combination of the `first` and `create` methods. This method will return an existing record if it already exists, but it will create them if it doesn't. As also apparent from the preceding code, we can supply a block into this method to assign the newly-created user with attributes of our choosing.

There's one caveat with the `first_or_create` method, though, because it contains the `create` method that does all the validations and persists in the database. Thus, we must be prepared if this method fails when doing validations or when saving our user in the database. Let's handle it in our controller by checking whether the user is successfully persisted by the `persisted?` method supplied by `ActiveRecord`.

```
class OmniauthCallbacksController < Devise::OmniauthCallbacksControll
er
  def twitter
    user = User.process_omniauth(request.env["omniauth.auth"])
    if user.persisted?
      flash.notice = "Signed in!"
      sign_in_and_redirect user
    else
      session["devise.user_attributes"] = user.attributes
      redirect_to new_user_registration_url
    end
  end
end
```

If the user hasn't been persisted, it means that the `first_or_create` method, which was called, failed in saving the user in the database. Therefore, we redirect our user into the new user registration form to correct any mistakes that may occur during this automated process. However, we must store the attributes somewhere to make sure that the form is preloaded with authentication information, which we got from Twitter; so, let's store it in the session with the `devise.user_attributes` key.

We must tell Devise to automatically preload forms with attributes that were stored in the session if these attributes are available. To do this, we can override Devise's `new_with_session` class method in our `User` model. This override checks whether the session information with the `devise.user_attributes` key exists. If it does, it will assign the attributes automatically. It will also assign attributes from `params` if it's available, and run the validation so that error messages will instantly pop up when the user opens the form.

```
def self.new_with_session(params, session)
  if session["devise.user_attributes"]
    new(session["devise.user_attributes"], without_protection: true)
do |user|
      user.attributes = params
      user.valid?
    end
  else
    super
  end
end
```

At this point, we will actually have a fully working authentication system, which uses remote authentication to verify user credentials. However, our application still has problems that need to be ironed out. Devise will still prompt that users have to supply a password when submitting their registration form, although it isn't necessary anymore as now they can use remote authentication. To change this behavior, we can override Devise's `password_required?` method so that Devise can skip password validation if the `provider` field isn't blank:

```
def password_required?
  super && provider.blank?
end
```

While we're at it, let's also modify Devise's registration form so that the password-related fields won't show up when our users use remote authentication. We can find the registration form at `app/views/devise/registrations/new.html.erb`. If you can't find it, you may have to execute `rails generate devise:views` first.

```
<h2>Sign up</h2>

<%= form_for(resource, :as => resource_name, :url => registration_
path(resource_name)) do |f| %>
  <%= devise_error_messages! %>

  <div class="field"><%= f.label :email %><br />
  <%= f.email_field :email %></div>

  <div class="field"><%= f.label :username %><br />
  <%= f.text_field :username %></div>

  <% if f.object.password_required? %>
    <div class="field"><%= f.label :password %><br />
    <%= f.password_field :password %></div>

    <div class="field"><%= f.label :password_confirmation %><br />
    <%= f.password_field :password_confirmation %></div>
  <% end %>

  <div class="field"><%= f.submit "Sign up" %></div>
<% end %>

<%= render "devise/shared/links" %>
```

Another problem that needs to be tackled, is when a user wants to modify his/her profile, they will have to supply their current password, which will be validated by Devise. We have to override this behavior, because some of our users won't have passwords anymore. We can override Devise's `update_with_password` method in our `User` model to achieve this:

```
def update_with_password(params, *options)
  if encrypted_password.blank? && provider.present?
    update_attributes(params, *options)
  else
    super
  end
end
```

Let's hide the `current_password` field in the profile-editing page (`app/views/devise/registrations/edit.html.erb`) for when users do not have any password.

```
<% if f.object.encrypted_password.present? %>
  <div class="field"><%= f.label :current_password %> <i>(we need your current password to confirm your changes)</i><br />
  <%= f.password_field :current_password %></div>
<% end %>
```

After we finished with the last step, we will have completed adding support for remote authentication using Twitter. Now, we can carry onto the next step, which is to add support for Facebook authentication. This will be easier, because we already have the logic for carrying remote authentication in place.

Remote authentication using Facebook

The steps for adding support for remote authentication using Facebook into our application is quite similar to the steps that we have taken when adding Twitter support. We also have to register our application at the Facebook developer site to get `APP_ID` and `APP_SECRET`, which we will use in our application.

Let's start the process by registering our application at the Facebook developer site.

Registering our application at the Facebook developer site

To register our application, we can go to `https://developers.facebook.com/`. Of course, we have to already have a Facebook account so that we can sign in to this site. If not, we have to sign up first.

After a successful sign-in, we can click on the **Apps** menu on the top of our screen, which will take us into our dashboard:

Then, we can click on **Create new app** to register our application. We will be presented with a form that contains the basic information about our application that we have to fill in. Just make sure that the **App Name** and **App Namespace** fields are filled with unique names. If it's already taken, we will have to pick a different name.

Click on **Continue** to register your application.

We will be presented with our application dashboard on successful registration. We can also click on **Edit App** in our application dashboard to go to this page. The most important thing in this page is to write down the information for **App ID** and **App Secret**, which we will use later. We also have to check **Website with Facebook Login** in the **Select how your app integrates with Facebook** section. Don't forget to fill in the site URL with the usual **fully qualified domain name** (**FQDN**) of localhost (`http://127.0.0.1:3000/`). Obviously, you can change this into any domain name that will host your application:

Just remember that changes in the Facebook application dashboard will sometimes take several minutes to propagate. Just prepare early, be patient when something unexpected occurs, and try it again after several minutes have passed.

Now, after we get our **App ID** and **App Secret** information from Facebook, we can continue to configure our application to add the Facebook authentication support.

Configuring OmniAuth for authentication using Facebook

First, we have to tell Devise that we want to add support for OmniAuth Facebook authentication by modifying `config/initializers/devise.rb`. We must also specify the **App ID** and **App Secret** values that we got earlier here.

```
config.omniauth :facebook, 'APP_ID', 'APP_SECRET'
```

We already specified an action called `twitter` in our `OmniauthCallbacksController`. The logic within the `twitter` action can be reused by the Facebook authentication scheme. We can use Rails' `alias_method` to achieve that, so let's modify our code as follows:

```
class OmniauthCallbacksController < Devise::OmniauthCallbacksControll
er
  def provider
    user = User.process_omniauth(request.env["omniauth.auth"])
    if user.persisted?
      flash.notice = "Signed in!"
      sign_in_and_redirect user
    else
      session["devise.user_attributes"] = user.attributes
      redirect_to new_user_registration_url
    end
  end

  alias_method :twitter, :provider
  alias_method :facebook, :provider
end
```

Don't forget to put a link for our users to authenticate with Facebook in your sign-in page:

```
<div id="user_nav">
  <% if current_user %>
    Signed in as <strong><%= current_user.name %></strong>!
    <%= link_to "Sign out", signout_path, id: "sign_out" %>
  <% else %>
    <%= link_to "Sign in with Facebook", "/auth/facebook", id: "sign_
in" %>
  <% end %>
</div>
```

Actually, that was it for adding support for Facebook authentication. Adding support for Facebook is a lot easier, because we already have the logic in place when adding the Twitter authentication support. Of course, we can always make improvements to our application; the examples include support for scenarios where users can utilize multiprovider authentication in one account or support for LinkedIn and Google authentication.

Summary

By completing the guidance provided in this chapter, we will have successfully created an application that can authenticate its users using remote authentication with third-party providers. To explore this topic further, you can try to implement support for providers other than Twitter and Facebook, which was described in this chapter.

Another thing to explore is the database scheme and logic that was used in this chapter, which was created with an assumption that users can only have one remote authentication provider for their account. If they, say, want to sign in using a Facebook account or a Twitter account into the same account in our application, they won't be able to do so with the current configurations. To support that scheme, we may have to create a separate model for storing the `provider` and `uid` information. Our `User` model must also have a `has_many` relationship to this new model. Lastly, we also have to modify the logic in our application accordingly.

5
Testing Devise

Now, you have reached this point where you have learned so many things about Devise. You started by setting up Devise modules in your application and now you are already able to perform remote authentication with Devise. So, let's get to the next topic about testing your Devise.

Some people think, maybe even you, that in certain circumstances, testing is just wasting your time. Some of you may have little time to develop your application, and some of you may only have a little number of people in your team that you decide to focus on building the features without performing any automated tests. It's not wrong at all, but I think the main concept of automated tests is about costing you time in the beginning of the development phase and saving a lot of your time in the future. So, we can say, this act is a kind of preventive action.

There are many kinds of testing, such as unit testing, integration testing, and functional testing. We are going to perform unit and functional testing. In Ruby on Rails, unit testing is performed to test your model and functional testing is performed to test your controller. I'm not going to write the definitions and other details for unit and functional testing, which means, when you read this chapter, it is required that you know the definition of these tests and how they are used in Ruby on Rails. To learn more about tests in Ruby on Rails, you can visit `http://guides.rubyonrails.org/testing.html`.

In this chapter, I'm going to give you some examples of tests that you can perform on your application. The examples are as follows:

- The sign-up test
- The user update test
- The user deletion test
- The sign-in test
- The remote authentication test

Why do you pick these five actions as examples? Didn't you give us a lot of examples between user deletion test and remote authentication test? These are good questions. I picked these as examples because I think these actions are basic authentications that you need to grab before you advance to the next level, that is, testing the customized Devise modules.

As for your information, by default, we are going to use the default testing tool provided by Ruby on Rails (Test::Unit). However, to expand your knowledge about testing tools, we are going to use **RSpec** (`http://rspec.info/`) and **Factory Girl** (`https://github.com/thoughtbot/factory_girl`) for the **Remote authentication test**.

As I mentioned before, Ruby on Rails provides a default test, which we can use. I'm going to use this for example one until four; therefore, we need to make some preparations. The first thing that you need to provide is a test fixture (`http://guides.rubyonrails.org/testing.html#the-low-down-on-fixtures`). You can open a file located under the `test/fixtures/` folder. If you already generated a model (let's call it the `user` model), you will have `users.yml` under that folder. Now, please define one data at least within the fixture. The following is an example of `users.yml`:

```
one:
  email: hafizbadrie@gmail.com
  encrypted_password:
    $2a$10$zhKHXP2NlENyYuaYCtwS.e6SfekdVG3Q78qINVgY6Wg4A6c5HknSW
  username: hafizbadrie
```

This test also requires some Devise specifications, which are stated in the previous chapters; so, I won't repeat the setup explanation in this chapter. In the next step, you have to configure your database for the test environment and perform this command to create a test database and migrate the tables as follows:

```
$> rake db:create
$> rake db:migrate RAILS_ENV=test
```

The sign-up test

Sign-up is the first action that you need to test. Why? Because if people can't sign up at your application, then sign-in and any other authentication will be useless. This is actually a simple test. You just need to add new data to the user table and check whether it's inserted or not. To do this, please open `test/models/user_test.rb` and add this code inside the `UserTest` class:

```
test "sign up" do
user = User.new({
:email => "hafizbadrie@hotmail.com",
```

```
:username => "hafizblubis",
:password => "devisetest",
:password_confirmation => "devisetest"
})

assert user.save, "User not signed up!"
end
```

The previous code will try to insert new data and check whether it's inserted or not with `assert user.save, "User not signed up!"` If it isn't, the message written will show up. Now, let's try and run our first Devise test by executing the following command:

```
$> rake test
```

The result of the test is similar to the following screenshot:

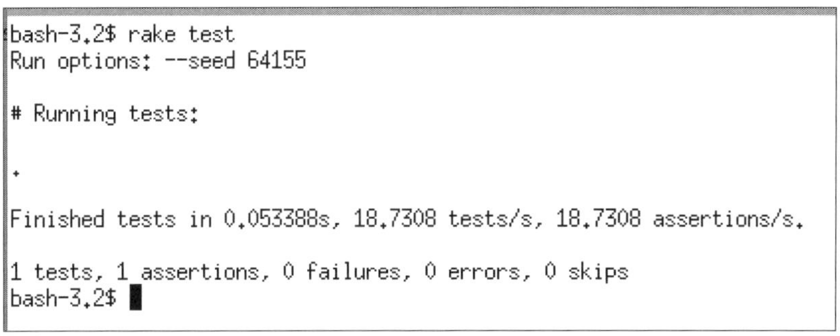

The sign-up testing result

As you can see, you currently have one test and this test performs one assertion. You also have no failures or errors, which means the result is as per our expectation.

The user update test

You already have one test in your model test and now we are going to add one more test; it is the user update test. We're going to perform two kinds of scenarios for this test:

- Update the user account without a password: Please open and modify `test/models/user_test.rb` and add this code inside the class:

  ```
  test "user edit without password" do
  user = User.first
  new_data = {
  :email => "hafizbadrie@gmail.com",
  ```

```
:username => "hafizlubis"
}
new_data = ActionController::Parameters.new(new_data)
new_data = new_data.permit(:email, :username)
user.update_without_password(new_data)

assert_equal user.username, 'hafizlubis', "User is not updated"
end
```

The first line inside the test code tries to get the data from the fixture and store it to a variable. Based on my fixture, I have data that has, `hafizbadrie@gmail.com`, as the e-mail and `hafizbadrie` as the username. I intend to update the username to hafizlubis and check whether it's updated with an assertion or not. You can see the result of the test in the following screenshot:

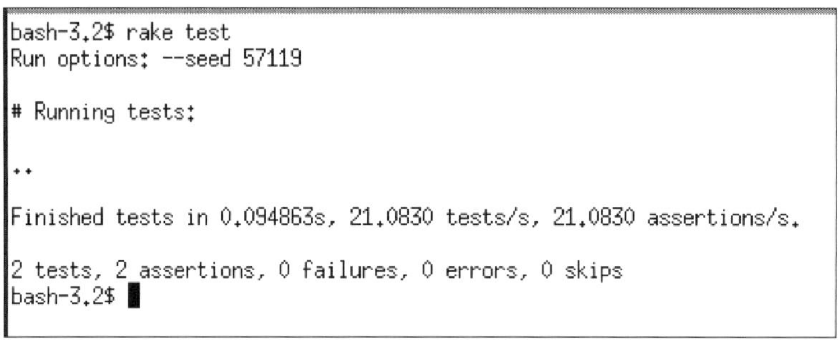

The user update without password test

Congratulations! Your test has succeeded once more since you have no failures and errors. The simulation data is successfully loaded and updated.

- **Update the user account with a password**: To test your user update along with its password, you need to use a different method name; that is, `update_with_password`. Let's see the following code example:

```
test "user edit with password" do
user = User.first
new_data = {
:username => "hafizlubis",
:current_password => "hafizmelulu",
:password => "devisetest",
:password_confirmation => "devisetest"
}
new_data = ActionController::Parameters.new(new_data)
new_data = new_data.permit(:email, :username, :current_password,
:password, :password_confirmation)
```

```
user.update_with_password(new_data)

assert_equal user.username, 'hafizlubis', "Password is not
updated"
end
```

This code is inserted within the class, which is also located at `test/models/user_test.rb`. I intend to update the password and username of an existing account with the username `hafizbadrie`, so I will change the account's password and then call the `update_with_password` method to save these changes. To check whether the test is successful or not, I will make an assertion against the updated username. The result of this test is shown in the following screenshot:

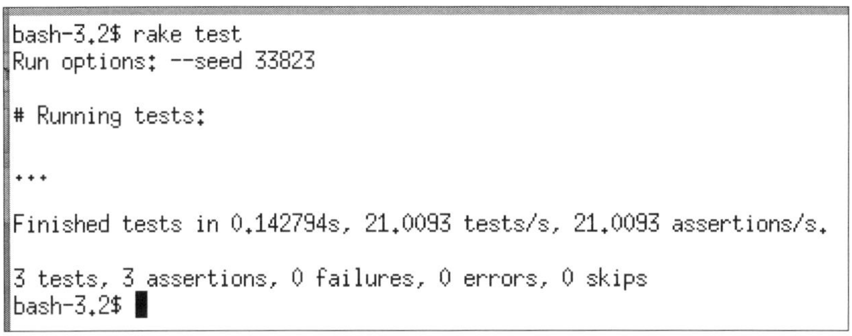

The user update with password test

If your test passes all test cases with all assertions returning the expected values, this means your data for simulation is successfully changing the previous passwords.

The user deletion test

This example will show you how to apply a test for user deletion. We are going to pass through a simple case in our test case. Now, let's modify your `user_test.rb` file so that it contains the following code within its class:

```
test "user deletion" do
user = User.first
user.destroy
deleted_user = User.first

assert deleted_user.nil?, "User is not deleted"
end
```

You have prepared the test case. Let's execute it. The result will be as shown in the following screenshot:

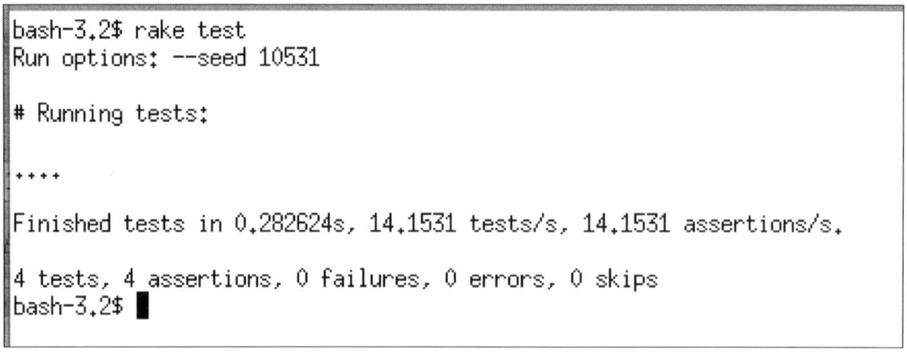

The user deletion test

When you see this result in your console, it means you have passed all your test cases.

The sign-in test

Now, we will see how to perform the sign-in test. In this case, we will no longer use unit testing, and perform functional testing instead. This test will be performed at the controller test file and we start by testing the authentication filter. We expect that when users visit the index action of the user's controller, they will be redirected to the Devise sign-in page. To do it, please open and modify `test/controllers/users_controller_test.rb`. Add the following code inside the `UsersControllerTest` class:

```
include Devise::TestHelpers

test "should be redirected" do
get :index
assert_redirected_to new_user_session_path, "User is not redirected!"
end
```

Don't forget to include `Devise::TestHelpers` because we are going to use some Devise helpers such as `authenticate` and `sign_in`. Both these methods are defined in this class. The test code will make a request to the index action of the user's controller. Since we expect that users will be redirected to the sign-in page, we are going to make an assertion named `assert_redirected_to`. If the redirected page is not as we expected, the fail message will show up.

You can see the result of the test in the following screenshot:

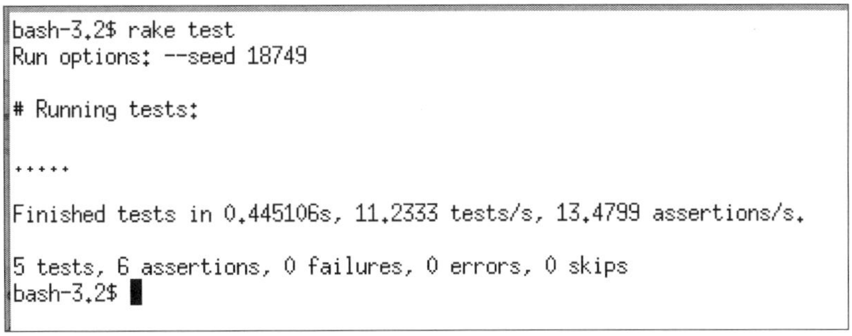

The user redirection test

All the tests have passed without any errors, so we are going to continue to the next test, which is the sign-in test. To perform this test, please add the following code inside `test/controllers/users_controller_test.rb`:

```
test "should sign in"  do
@request.env["devise.mapping"] = Devise.mappings[:user]

user = User.first
sign_in user

get :index
assert_response :success, "User is not signed in!"
end
```

This test will try to perform sign-in of an account and check whether it's succeeded or not. To validate it, we'll try visiting the index action of `users_controller_test`. If we are redirected to another page, this means the Devise filter is executed because there is not a single signed-in account. However, if we get the actual page of the index action, this means we have successfully signed in. To perform this test, we need to use `sign_in` and `assert_response` methods. The `sign_in` Devise helper is used to perform the Devise sign-in action and `assert_response` is used to see the response code from the server. For this test, we use `:success`, which defines code 200.

The Remote authentication test

As I mentioned before, for this test, we will use a different testing tool called RSpec and Factory Girl.

> *RSpec is a testing tool for the Ruby programming language. Born under the banner of Behavior-Driven Development, it is designed to make Test-Driven Development a productive and enjoyable experience (*`http://rspec.info/`*).*
>
> *factory_girl is a fixtures replacement with a straightforward definition syntax, support for multiple build strategies (saved instances, unsaved instances, attribute hashes, and stubbed objects), and support for multiple factories for the same class (user, admin_user, and so on), including factory inheritance (*`https://github.com/thoughtbot/factory_girl`*).*

In this condition, we are going to replace the default test framework with RSpec and fixtures with Factory Girl. This means you will have methods different from the previous examples and, as a consequence, you will learn a new method for performing tests. Eventually, you will be able to compare which testing tool is more suitable for you.

To start our test with RSpec and Factory Girl, we need to add both gems in our `Gemfile` as follows:

```
group :development, :test do
gem 'rspec-rails', '~> 2.14.0'
gem 'factory_girl_rails', '~> 4.2.1'
end
```

If you haven't installed these gems in your gemset, you can run the `bundle install` command before proceeding to the next steps. Next, you should initialize RSpec by executing the following command:

```
$> rails generate rspec:install
```

The result of the previous command is shown in the following screenshot:

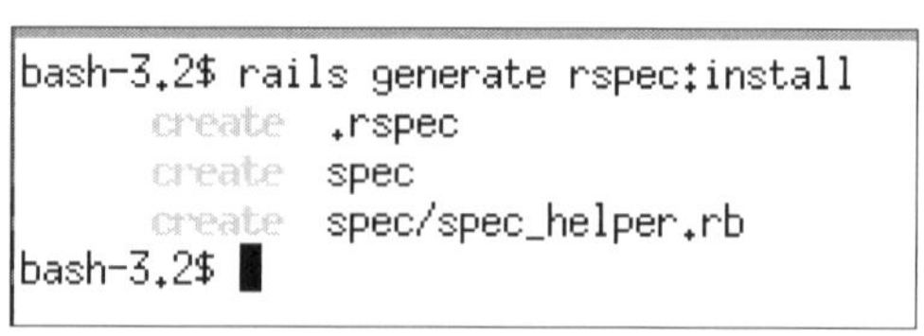

The RSpec installation result

Let's continue by preparing Factory Girl for your test. Since you already have the `spec` folder, please add a new folder named `factories` under it. We will put our `factories` file under it. To apply our new testing tool as our test default, you need to add some extra configuration to your generator. You can do this by modifying your `config/application.rb` file and adding the following code:

```
config.generators do |g|
g.test_framework :rspec, :fixture => true
g.fixture_replacement :factory_girl, :dir => "spec/factories"
end
```

Before we proceed to the next step, you should pay attention to the configuration in the `spec/spec_helper.rb` file. We are going to tell Rails not to use its default fixtures. To do this, please open the file and include the following two lines:

```
config.fixture_path = "#{::Rails.root}/spec/fixtures"
config.user_transactional_fixtures = true
```

Therefore, our new testing tool will become the default tool for testing. If you start this test from a brand new project, the application will automatically generate RSpec files when you execute `rails generate model` and `rails generate controller` commands. However, if you start installing this testing tool with controllers and models that are already generated, you will need to add some files by yourself. Since this example uses the code written in *Chapter 4, Remote Authentication with Devise and OmniAuth*, you need to add some test files in the `spec` folder.

This test will show you two kinds of tests: a functional test performed in the controller and a unit test performed in the model. However, before we start the test, we have to prepare our fixture defined by Factory Girl. Please execute the following command to produce a file named `users.rb`, which is located at `spec/factories/`:

```
$ rails generate factory_girl:model User email username provider uid
```

Now, open the file and modify it so that the code will look like the following lines of code.

```
require 'factory_girl_rails'

FactoryGirl.define do
factory :user do
email 'learningdeviseforrails@gmail.com'
username 'hafizbadrie'
provider 'twitter'
uid '1234567'
end
end
```

Now, let's start writing our test code from the unit test. Please add a new file named `users_spec.rb` under `spec/models/`. If you don't have a folder named `models`, you can create it on your own and save the file under that folder. Referring to the `user.rb` file written in *Chapter 4, Remote Authentication with Devise and OmniAuth*, we have a method called `process_omniauth`, and we will create our test case in that method. Please write the following code inside `users_spec.rb`:

```
require 'spec_helper'

describe User do
it "processes omniauth from existing user" do
auth = {
:provider => "twitter",
:uid => "1234567",
:info => {
:nickname => "hafizbadrie"
}
}
user = FactoryGirl.create(:user)
tested_user = User.process_omniauth(auth)

expect(tested_user).to eq(user)
end

it "processes omniauth with new user" do
auth = {
:provider => "twitter",
:uid => "1234567",
:info => {
:nickname => "hafizbadrie"
}
}
tested_user = User.process_omniauth(auth)
expect(tested_user.persisted?).to be_false
end
end
```

You just defined two test cases for the `process_omniauth` method. The first test case shows that the method processing the data defined by `auth` is equal to the data existing in the database, while the second shows the opposite of this, that is, the data defined by `auth` is new. As you can see, the method used by RSpec is different from the ones we used in previous examples. For more information about the methods, you can go to the following original documentation sites:

- `http://rubydoc.info/gems/rspec-core`
- `http://rubydoc.info/gems/rspec-expectations`

- `http://rubydoc.info/gems/rspec-mocks`
- `http://rubydoc.info/gems/rspec-rails`

We have prepared the test case and now, it's time to execute it. Please run the following command to see the results:

```
$> rspec spec/models
```

You also can use the following command to execute all the tests you have (models, controllers, and the views test), which is slower than the previous command:

```
$> rake spec
```

The result will show that you have passed two examples, as shown in the following screenshot:

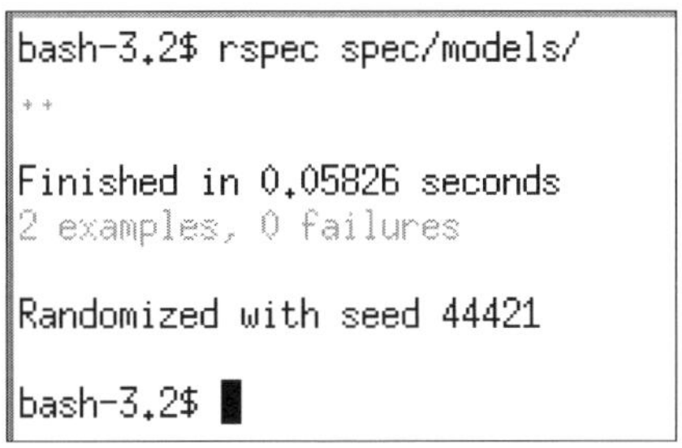

The unit test with RSpec result

Let's continue executing the functional test at our controller. Please create a file named `omniauth_callbacks_controller_spec.rb` under `spec/controllers`. If you already have the file, you can skip this step; however, if you don't, you have to create the folder and file on your own.

As described in *Chapter 4, Remote Authentication with Devise and OmniAuth* the `omniauth_callbacks_controller.rb` file provides an action named provider. The test will show two types of test cases. The first case will show the condition when a user signs in with a new Twitter or Facebook account. The second case will show the condition when a user signs in with an existing account via Twitter or Facebook. The following is the example test code that I wrote:

```
require 'spec_helper'

describe OmniauthCallbacksController do
before(:each) do
request.env["omniauth.auth"] = {
:uid => "1234567",
:provider => "twitter",
```

```
:info => {
:nickname => "hafizbadrie"
}
}
end

describe "GET #provider" do
it "sign up with twitter success" do
user = User.new
get :twitter
response.should redirect_to new_user_registration_url
end

it "twitter sign in success" do
user = FactoryGirl.create(:user)
get :twitter
response.should redirect_to root_path
end
end
end
```

The previous code gives you two cases. The first case shows that the user should be redirected to the registration page because the incoming user is a new user. The second case uses the data defined in our factory to sign in and then the user should be redirected to the root path defined in the route. Please remember that to run the test perfectly, you have to create a dummy value for `omniauth.auth`, which is used by the `process_omniauth`. In the previous code, the dummy value is defined in the `before(:each) ... do` block of code, which is executed in every test case.

Now, let's see the result of the test. Please execute `rspec spec/controllers` and the result will be as follows:

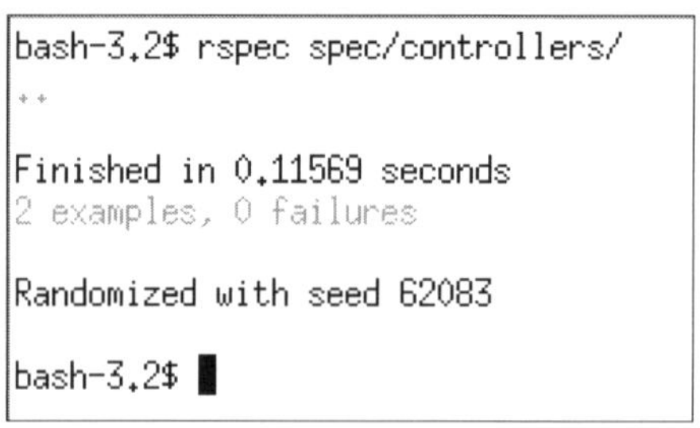

The Functional test with RSpec

In the example, I wrote a case where the user signs in with a Twitter account. So, what about a Facebook account? You can apply the same test with a Facebook account with minor changes. First, you should change the provider value in `request.env["omniauth.auth"]` from `twitter` to `facebook`. In every test case, you should replace `get :twitter` with `get :facebook`. This should do it and the test will be performed with Facebook as its provider.

Summary

In this chapter you have learned about how to test some of the Devise actions. Some of them are performed with the default Ruby on Rails testing tool and some use RSpec and Factory Girl. With different testing tools being used in the examples, you are expected to be able to compare which tool is more suitable for you. The test itself is meant to make your Devise and application more solid and less faulty. As I have said earlier, you may think that this activity will consume some of your time, which could be allocated to developing other features, or you can say that developers can perform the test manually. However, as the application grows, developers will start losing track of the bugs they have exterminated and tests they have performed. Repeating the same test manually will be more inefficient. The point is that depending on the size of your application, you may choose whether to apply the test or not, but the end point of the development should remain the same; that is, to develop a useful and solid application.

Index

Symbols

A

B

C

D

E

F

H

L

M

N

U

V

W

Thank you for buying

Learning Devise for Rails

About Packt Publishing

Packt, pronounced 'packed', published its first book "*Mastering phpMyAdmin for Effective MySQL Management*" in April 2004 and subsequently continued to specialize in publishing highly focused books on specific technologies and solutions.

Our books and publications share the experiences of your fellow IT professionals in adapting and customizing today's systems, applications, and frameworks. Our solution based books give you the knowledge and power to customize the software and technologies you're using to get the job done. Packt books are more specific and less general than the IT books you have seen in the past. Our unique business model allows us to bring you more focused information, giving you more of what you need to know, and less of what you don't.

Packt is a modern, yet unique publishing company, which focuses on producing quality, cutting-edge books for communities of developers, administrators, and newbies alike. For more information, please visit our website: `www.packtpub.com`.

About Packt Open Source

In 2010, Packt launched two new brands, Packt Open Source and Packt Enterprise, in order to continue its focus on specialization. This book is part of the Packt Open Source brand, home to books published on software built around Open Source licences, and offering information to anybody from advanced developers to budding web designers. The Open Source brand also runs Packt's Open Source Royalty Scheme, by which Packt gives a royalty to each Open Source project about whose software a book is sold.

Writing for Packt

We welcome all inquiries from people who are interested in authoring. Book proposals should be sent to `author@packtpub.com`. If your book idea is still at an early stage and you would like to discuss it first before writing a formal book proposal, contact us; one of our commissioning editors will get in touch with you.

We're not just looking for published authors; if you have strong technical skills but no writing experience, our experienced editors can help you develop a writing career, or simply get some additional reward for your expertise.

OpenAM

ISBN: 978-1-849510-22-6 Paperback: 292 pages

Written and tested with OpenAM Snapshot 9 - the Single Sign-On (SSO) tool for securing your web applications in a fast and easy way

1. The first and the only book that focuses on implementing Single Sign-On using OpenAM
2. Learn how to use OpenAM quickly and efficiently to protect your web applications with the help of this easy-to-grasp guide
3. Written by Indira Thangasamy, core team member of the OpenSSO project from which OpenAM is derived

---

Railo 3 Beginner's Guide

ISBN: 978-1-849513-40-1 Paperback: 364 pages

Easily develop and deploy complex applications online using the powerful Railo Server

1. A complete guide to developing an application with Railo from start to finish
2. In depth coverage of installing Railo Server on different environments
3. A detailed look ORM, AJAX, Flex and other technologies to boost your development

Please check **www.PacktPub.com** for information on our titles

[PACKT] open source
community experience distilled
PUBLISHING

Ruby on Rails Enterprise Application Development: Plan, Program, Extend

ISBN: 978-1-847190-85-7 Paperback: 528 pages

Building a complete Ruby on Rails business application from start to finish

1. Create a non-trivial, business-focused Rails application
2. Solve the real-world problems of developing and deploying Rails applications in a business environment

---

Aptana RadRails: An IDE for Rails Development

ISBN: 978-1-847193-98-8 Paperback: 248 pages

Over 80 practical, task-based recipes to create applications using Boost libraries

1. Comprehensive guide to using RadRails during the whole development cycle
2. Code Assistance, Graphical Debugger, Testing, Integrated Console
3. Manage your gems, plug-ins, servers, generators, and Rake tasks

Please check **www.PacktPub.com** for information on our titles

3363960R00062

Printed in Germany
by Amazon Distribution
GmbH, Leipzig